THIS IS A CARLTON BOOK

This revised edition published in 2017
by Carlton Books Limited,
an imprint of Carlton Publishing Group,
20 Mortimer Street, London, WIT 3JW

Text and design © Carlton Books 2016

Author: Clive Gifford
Editor: Anna Brett
Art Editor: Dani Lurie
Design: Jake da'Costa & WildPixel Ltd.
Cover Design: WildPixel Ltd.
Production: Charlotte Larcombe
Picture Research: Steve Behan

All rights reserved.

No part of this publication may be reproduced or
distributed in any form or by any means without
the written permission of the copyright owner.

Printed in Dubai

9 8 7 6 5 4 3 2 1

ISBN: 978-1-78312-297-4

CLIVE GIFFORD

GAMING

RECORD BREAKERS

WINNING STREAKS!

HIGHEST SCORES!

MOST DOWNLOADS!

CARLTON KiDS

CONTENTS

NOTE TO READERS: FACTS AND STATS ARE ACCURATE UP TO APRIL 2017

THE GLORY OF GAMING

Welcome to the glorious world of gaming! This book is packed with all sorts of eye-popping records from marathon game sessions that resulted in world-record high scores, to the bestselling games and consoles, magical milestones and fantastic firsts in gaming. Whether you're potty for Pokémon GO or mad for Minecraft, this book is for you!

FOR ALL AGES

Gaming is not only for girls as well as boys, it's for all ages as well. According to the Entertainment Software Association the average age of a gamer in the USA is 35 years old. Bearing in mind millions of kids are avid gamers, that must mean that plenty of parents and grandparents enjoy gaming as well. In fact, over a quarter of all gamers in the USA are over 50 years of age.

NUMBER OF GAMERS BY REGION IN 2016

ASIA-PACIFIC	1,053 million
EUROPE	337 million
AFRICA & MIDDLE EAST	301 million
SOUTH AMERICA	209 million
NORTH AMERICA	198 million

BESTSELLING CONSOLE

Many consoles quickly come and go as new and improved games machines arrive on the scene. One console, though, has outsold all others and is still enjoyed by many gamers to this day – the Sony PlayStation 2 (PS2). Since its release in 2000 more than 155 million have been sold – that's more than one each for the combined populations of Canada, Spain and France!

$ IN DEMAND

The PS2 was launched in Japan in March 2000 and caused a sensation. Around US$250 million worth of consoles, games and peripherals were sold on the first day alone! Demand was huge and some people paid three or four times the retail price of the console on auction sites like eBay.

$ DUALSHOCK

The PS2 came with Dualshock 2 game controllers. They featured two control sticks and pressure sensitive buttons, meaning the harder you pushed the stick, the stronger the action in the game.

$ HOT HARDWARE

The PS2 only had 32MB of memory and used 8MB memory cards to store information on, but it out-performed many of the competing consoles of the time. The machine also doubled as a DVD player and in Brazil offered Netflix movies and TV streaming if linked up to an Internet connection.

$ A LONG RUNNER

The PS2 was so popular that it kept on being made long after its successor, the PS3, was launched in 2006. In fact, it continued to be built by Sony until January 2013, making it one of the longest-produced consoles of all time.

The PS2 slimline version was launched in 2004.

$ GAMES GLUT

Compatible with the games of its predecessor, the Sony PlayStation, the PS2 built up a huge library of playable titles – over 10,000 in total. An estimated 1.52 billion games for the PS2 were sold by 2012. Among the console's bestsellers are Gran Turismo 4 with sales of 11.76 million and its predecessor GT3, which sold a massive 14.89 million copies.

One gamer from Banbury in the UK, Dan Holmes, loved his PS2 so much that in 2002 he changed his name by law to Mr PlayStation 2. Bonkers!

$ MORE THAN MEETS THE EYE

Released in 2003, the EyeToy was one of the first motion-sensing gaming cameras. This camera connected with the PS2 and could detect gestures made by the gamers to perform actions in a range of dedicated games. More than 10 million copies of this pioneering peripheral were sold.

FIRST COMPUTER GAMES

Imagine what it must have been like in the past. Thirty years ago there were no websites, fifty years ago there were no games consoles and seventy years ago there were next-to-no computers. The first games that did emerge on the earliest computers may have been primitive but they helped pave the way for gaming today.

1 BERTIE THE BRAIN

In 1950, at the Canadian National Exhibition, a 4m (13ft) tall machine wowed the crowd by being able to play noughts and crosses (tic-tac-toe) against a human opponent and win most of the time.

1 TENNIS FOR TWO

American physicist William Higinbotham developed a simple tennis simulation game at the Brookhaven National Laboratory in 1958. The game displayed a side-on view of the ball, bats and tennis net on an oscilloscope.

There was a special offer of six extra games for free if you bought an Odyssey before December 1974!

Give the gift that makes TV more than something they just sit and watch: Odyssey.

ODYSSEY
Electronic TV games from Magnavox.

1 THE FIRST GAMES CONSOLE

Ralph Baer had first suggested building a TV set which could play games as far back as 1951, but his bosses at Loral Electronics rejected the idea. Baer kept thinking about it, though, and in 1967 created the Brown Box, a console that plugged into a TV to play several simple games. Baer's invention was revised and eventually went on sale as the Magnavox Odyssey in 1972. Around 330,000 were sold.

Bertie the Brain, as it was nicknamed, signalled its move by switching on a light bulb in each of the grid's nine squares.

The Magnavox Odyssey came with 12 games including American football, card games and a simple ice hockey game all in black and white. The console came with see-through coloured overlays you could place over the TV screen to simulate colour graphics!

1 FIRST PERIPHERAL FOR A CONSOLE

Ralph Baer also designed the first optional gaming peripheral. Designed for the Magnavox Odyssey, the Shooting Gallery was a rifle-shaped light gun that could be used to fire at the TV screen when playing shooting games such as Dogfight and Shootout.

Early computer pioneers found that their machines were good at making lots of maths calculations very quickly and could analyze all the possible moves in board games such as chess or checkers. In 1951 a simple checkers-playing program was created.

FIRST ARCADE GAME

When you think of arcade games, you think of colourful all-action games played in bright, noisy arcades packed with machines. But the very first action game was written and played at a university, the Massachusetts Institute of Technology, or MIT. Spacewar! was first played way back in 1962.

BRIGHT SPARKS

MIT's Electrical Engineering Department had a PDP-1 computer that cost US$120,000 but which staff and students were allowed to use. Steve Russell, a young computer programmer at MIT, dreamt up the idea of a space battle game that featured two spaceships firing at each other. He and his colleagues then spent over 200 hours turning it into a reality.

INSPIRING IDEA

Spacewar! proved popular and spread to the handful of other places that had a PDP-1 computer. One of these was the University of Utah where a student, Nolan Bushnell, notched up hours of game time. In 1970-71, Bushnell worked with Ted Dabney and the pair developed their own space arcade game. They sold their version, called Computer Space, to Nutting Associates who built more than 1,500 machines in 1971. It was the first commercial computer games machine to appear in arcades.

Computer Space displayed a player's scores but only up to 15. If a player scored a further point, their score would reset to zero!

Spacewar! features two players who each control a spaceship, one shaped like a needle, the other shaped like a wedge. The aim is to blast the other out of space.

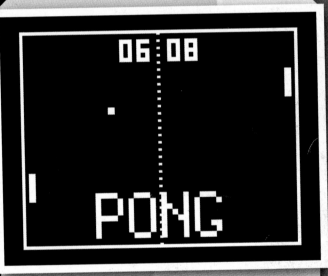

06:08

PONG

PONG!

Bushnell and Dabney formed Atari in 1972 with just US$500. The pair, along with engineer Allan Alcorn, produced the first sports arcade game using a TV and a milk carton to catch coins entered into the machine. The game was a simple tennis bat and ball game called Pong, and it proved to be a big hit with over 30,000 machines being sold into arcades.

Atari game designer Steve Wozniak, with fellow employees Steve Jobs and Ronald Wayne, went on to form the computer company Apple in 1976.

digital CORPORATION

SPACE INVADERS

High scores first featured in mid-1970s arcade games, but they were only a target to gain gamers bonus play-time. Taito's Space Invaders was the brainchild of Tomohiro Nishikado. He designed the graphics, gameplay and even the game's circuits. When it debuted in 1978, it was the first to save the highest score and display it on screen.

EXPORTED AND PORTED

News of this new game was passed on by word of mouth, and sales boomed. Taito in Japan and Midway in the USA went on to sell around 360,000 cabinets between them, making it the second most popular arcade game of all time (behind Pac-Man). Its popularity really exploded, though, when it was ported to the Atari 2600 home games console in 1980 and it became the first game to sell over one million cartridges.

Five waves of aliens march slowly across and down the screen.

Barriers at the bottom provide shelter until they are destroyed by the aliens.

SPACE INVADERS DATA

CREATOR	Tomohiro Nishikado, Taito
PUBLISHER	Taito, Midway
LAUNCH	1978
TYPE	Space shooter
MAJOR PLATFORMS	Arcade, Atari 2600, Various since

Nishikado designed the aliens to look like crabs, squid and other underwater creatures.

SHOOT 'EM UP FIRSTS

Space Invaders also included other innovations. It was the first shooter game where the targets shot back, the first where players had more than one life and also the first arcade game to feature barriers that were gradually destroyed by the aliens' fire. Its continuous soundtrack of simple bass beeps that speeded up was also a notable first.

TAKE A BREAK

Released a year after the original, Deluxe Space Invaders was the first game to introduce a short break between each level after it was completed. It also added a command ship which, if hit, gained the gamer a 500-point bonus and allowed a player achieving a high score to add his name beside it.

A player's laser destroys the aliens, but the more that are destroyed, the faster the remaining aliens move.

SUPER SCORE

The record score on the classic version of Space Invaders was set at 55,160 in 2003 by Donald Hayes and then smashed eight years later by Richie Vavrence, better known as Richie Knucklez, with a huge high score of 110,510.

SUPER HIGH SCORE

In November 1982, 15-year-old Scott Safran popped a quarter (25 US cent) coin into the slot of an Atari Asteroids console at the All American Billiard Arcade in Newtown, Pennsylvania and 60 hours later had entered the record books. His mega marathon resulted in the world record asteroids high score of 41,336,440. It was a score that wouldn't be beaten for 28 years!

According to Retro Gamer Magazine, over US$500 million has been spent playing games of Asteroids in arcades.

SPACE SUCCESS

More than 70,000 Asteroids machines found their way into arcades but the game reached an even bigger fanbase when it was ported to the Atari 2600 games console and sold an estimated 3.8 million copies. Since that time, dozens of official and unofficial clones of the game have found their way on to all sorts of computing and gaming systems.

Asteroids calls on you to move and rotate your spaceship to blast away at asteroids large and small which drift across the screen and can smash your ship if you're not careful. Players start the game with three lives.

RECORD BUSTER

In 2010 a 41-year-old locksmith from Seattle, John McAllister, broke Safran's record using an Asteroids console in his friend's basement in Portland, Oregon. McAllister scored 41,338,740 points in a 58-hour marathon that was live streamed on Justin.TV. Without a pause button, McAllister had to rush for toilet breaks and to grab a sandwich.

LOW HIGH SCORE

Some arcade games are very low scoring. Konami's Teenage Mutant Ninja Turtles: Turtles in Time is one example. Its world record high score is 212, achieved by American David Price in 2009 at a New York comics convention.

A bug in the arcade version of Missile Command means that if you reach a score of 810,000 you receive 176 bonus cities, greatly extending game time.

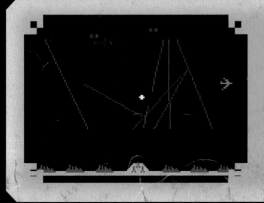

MISSILE COMMAND

Another Atari arcade game also possesses a stunning high score record, this time by Swede Victor Sandberg. In December 2013, Sandberg played for 71 hours and 41 minutes to reach level 10,432 of Missile Command, notching up an incredible score of 103,809,990!

EXPENSIVE MACHINES

Serious PC gamers spend plenty of money on their machines in an effort to get maximum performance. Gaming machines need powerful processors and graphics cards to run the latest graphic-intensive action games at high speeds. Top of the shop is the 8Pack OrionX. Released in February 2017, it costs a cool £24,000!

$ COOL COMPUTER

Designed by PC gaming legend Ian '8Pack' Perry, the 8Pack OrionX is actually two computers in one. Crammed into its US$900 case are two complete PCs. In total, they boast 14 CPU cores, three top-of-the-range GTX 980 Ti graphics cards and over 4TB of memory storage. The entire machine is cooled not by a fan blowing air as in most PCs, but by tubes of liquid carried around the machine.

$ ULTIMATE RACER

Gamers who specialize in car racing simulations often buy steering wheel and foot pedal controllers to make their experience more like real racing. The VRX Z-55 iMotion Racing Simulator takes this much, much further with 500 watts of surround sound blaring out of five speakers and a computer-controlled motor system fitted to the seat. This mimics engine and road vibrations as well as acceleration, braking and turning. It all comes at a cost, with prices starting at over £50,000!

The PC installed at the heart of the VRX Z-55 can run different racing games and simulations at a stunning speed of 240 frames of action per second.

Three 140-cm (55-in) screens on the VRX Z-55 display give an 180-degree view of the race for the gamer.

$ BACK IN THE DAY

Back in the 1990s, the most expensive games machine to hit the stores was the 3DO Interactive Multiplayer. Built by three companies – GoldStar, Sanyo and initially, in 1993, Panasonic – it was one of the first consoles to use CDs. The 3DO won Time magazine's product of the year award, but at US$699 it proved too expensive for many.

$ COSTLY CONSOLES

British designer Stuart Hughes has produced the world's most expensive games console. His Wii Supreme, only three of which were made, has a reformed cover made of more than 2,500g (88oz) of 22-carat gold and the front buttons are encrusted with a total of 78 diamonds. The price tag is an enormous £299,995!

Wii SPORTS

Nintendo's Wii console was an exciting development for casual gamers when it was launched in 2006. It has motion-sensing controllers that allow gamers to make realistic movements to control activities such as swinging a racket to play a sport. Bundled with the console was Wii Sports, a package containing five games: baseball, bowling, boxing, golf and tennis.

BOWLED OVER

Retired school headteacher John Bates bowled his way to Wii Sports glory from April 2009. By October 2010, he had recorded 2,850 perfect games (scores of 300), making the 83-year-old a world record holder. Bates continued his record-breaking run and in April 2015 he bowled his 20,000th perfect game.

The longest home run in Wii Sports' baseball game was struck by Brandon Christof in the Canadian town of Shakespeare in 2013. Christof smashed the ball a record distance of 204.83m (672ft).

SPORTS RESORT

Released three years after Wii Sports, Sports Resort was packed with 12 games including wakeboarding, archery and canoeing all played on the fictional Wuhu Island. The game was bundled with the improved Wii MotionPlus game controller which offered faster, more accurate gameplay - handy for Anthony Gertzos in September 2016 when he notched a world record 3,211 points in Sports Resort's wakeboarding game.

Nintendo has sold 32.99 million copies of Sports Resort since its release.

20

Wii SPORTS DATA

CREATOR	Nintendo Entertainment Analysis and Development No.2
PUBLISHER	Nintendo
LAUNCH	2006
TYPE	Sports
MAJOR PLATFORMS	Wii

In Wii tennis you earn skill points for winning points and games. Dozens of gamers are all tied for the highest proven number of skill points so far: 2,399 points.

TIME TO SWITCH

1-2-Switch is NIntendo's latest multi-sports and mini game pack, released in March 2017 for its brand-new Nintendo Switch console. Using twin Joy-Con controllers, players can battle each other at baseball, table tennis and swordfight duels among its 28 different games. More than 1.5 million Nintendo Switch consoles were sold within a week of its launch, making it Nintendo's fastest-selling console in both Europe and North America.

ONE OF A KIND

Some games are produced in special limited editions which may come with additional features or bonus products. These limited edition games can cost three or more times as much as the basic game. One limited edition game, the Mono Edition of GRID 2, goes much, much further. It costs an astonishing £125,000!

REALISTIC RACING

Released in 2013, GRID 2 is a sequel to the award-winning GRID. It's a racing game along circuits around the world, from the streets of Paris to the Collins Park Ring in Miami, USA and the Al Sufouh Strip in Dubai. It also features a wide range of cars from the gutsy Ford Mustang Mach 1 Twister Special to the powerful Aston Martin Vantage.

WHAT'S IN THE BOX?

The GRID 2 Mono Edition came with a PlayStation 3 console, a racing car helmet, an entire made-to-measure racing suit including boots and gloves... and a complete Briggs Automotive Company (BAC) Mono supercar! This single-seat racer, which features in the game, is made of carbon fibre and has a top speed of 270km/h (168mph).

The Mono Supercar goes from 0-96km/h

GRID 2 DATA

CREATOR	Ian Livingstone
PUBLISHER	Codemasters
LAUNCH	2013
TYPE	Car racing simulation
MAJOR PLATFORMS	PS3, Microsoft Windows, Xbox 360, Mac OS X

The Mono Edition even included a day out at the BAC factory setting up the supercar to the owner's preferences.

Deadmau5's real name is Joel Thomas Zimmerman.

🏎 ONE-OFF

Unlike many limited editions, the Mono Edition was a singular one-off. The Canadian musician and star DJ Deadmau5 bought the Mono Edition in 2014!

🏎 STICKS AND CATAPULTS

One of the most common limited editions was the Collector's Edition of the real-time strategy game Total War: Rome II, of which 22,000 copies were made. Costing US$400, it included the game, a scale model of a Roman Onager catapult and a campaign map printed on canvas.

165 km/h

000134

KING OF THE HANDHELDS

When it comes to handheld gaming fun, no company has built and sold more consoles than Japanese manufacturer Nintendo. Including its famous Game Boy, Nintendo has pioneered many generations of fun and feature-packed handheld games machines. In total, the company had sold 418.92 million handheld consoles by the end of 2016.

The Donkey Kong edition of Game & Watch released in 1982 was the first handheld game to feature the familiar cross-shaped D-pad as a direction controller.

New Super Mario Bros has sold over 30.8 million copies worldwide – the most popular DS game of all.

FROM CARDS TO CARTS

Founded in 1889, Nintendo originally produced Hanufada – a type of Japanese playing card – but branched out in the 1960s into instant rice meals and toys. A mechanic hired to repair factory machinery, Gunpei Yokoi, came up with the design of Nintendo's first handheld game, Game & Watch, in 1980. Some 59 different Game & Watch models were produced plus one limited-edition model.

The famous Louvre Museum in Paris, home of the Mona Lisa painting, uses Nintendo 3DS consoles to deliver its official tour guide to visitors.

DS IS BEST

Launched in 2004, the Nintendo DS was initially thought of as experimental but quickly caught on. It was the first handheld console with two screens, one of which was a touchscreen, as well as built-in Wi-Fi and a microphone. By the end of 2016 sales of DS models including DS Lite and DSi machines had reached 154.02 million, making it the most popular family of handheld consoles of all time.

GAME SALES FOR NINTENDO HANDHELDS (TO DEC 2016)

MILLIONS	CONSOLE
948.51	Nintendo DS
501.11	Game Boy
377.42	Game Boy Advance
320.96	Nintendo 3DS

VIRTUAL BOY

Not all Nintendo machines proved smash hits. The Virtual Boy offered users 3D graphics but the headset and battery pack were heavy and less than a million units were sold worldwide.

DANCE MARATHON

A primary school teacher from Bakersfield, California is the undisputed queen of dance gaming marathons. In July 2015, Carrie Swidecki managed to keep on dancing as she played Just Dance for an astonishing 138 hours and 34 seconds. She also holds ten marathon and 101 high score records on various dance games. Amazing!

JUST DANCE DATA

CREATOR	Ubisoft
PUBLISHER	Ubisoft
LAUNCH	2009
TYPE	Dancing rhythm game
MAJOR PLATFORMS	Wii, Wii U, PlayStation, Xbox 360, iOS, Android

TOP OF THE POPS

The Just Dance series is the biggest-selling family of dance games with sales of over 59 million copies by 2015. Just Dance gets its name from the Lady Gaga song. The song first featured in the fifth game of the series, Just Dance 2014, which was the first Xbox One- and PlayStation 4-compatible Just Dance game.

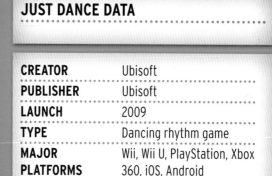

Just Dance 4 for the Wii U dispenses with a mat on the floor. Instead, gamers holding the Wii U dance and move to match the movements of the character on the screen.

DANCE DANCE REVOLUTION

Dance games first became popular in the late 1990s with the introduction of Konami's Dance Dance Revolution machine in arcades. Players stood on a dance platform and had to step on arrows which lit up on the platform in time with the music and instructions on screen. Carrie Swidecki first took up dance gaming on a Dance Dance Revolution arcade machine. Her longest marathon on the Supernova 2 version of the machine was a world record - 16 hours and 9 minutes in 2011.

Carrie was seriously overweight when she began dance gaming as a form of exercise. She has since lost over 34kg (75lb) in weight and supports the fight against childhood obesity.

WORLD CUP WINNER

Carrie took part in the first ever World Cup dancing competition in 2014, which was won by Brazil's Diego Dos Santos Silva. Diego won again in 2015 but lost the title at the next competition, which was held in Paris in 2017. Instead, it was 16-year-old Umutcan Tütüncü (above) from Turkey who triumphed to become the youngest World Cup winner.

DANCE DEVELOPMENTS

Following the success of Dance Dance Revolution, rival machines and games were produced, many designed for home games consoles. Dance Central uses the Kinect motion-sensing gaming device to track gamers' movements. Elizabeth Bolinger, who calls herself 'Kitty McScratch' and hails from Iowa, USA, holds over 100 high score records for songs on Dance Central and Just Dance.

EASTER EGGS

Easter eggs are secret added elements in a game. The first was found in a demo cartridge for the Fairchild Channel F console in 1976 and it displayed the name of the cartridge's programmer. Subsequent Easter eggs have been as simple as messages and jokes, up to complex unexpected levels and entire games hidden inside the original game.

GAME HELPERS

Some Easter eggs help players by giving them extra clues, lives or powers. In ToeJam & Earl, an alien action game originally for the Sega Genesis, there is a secret island level. it contains a hot tub which can heal a gamer's character and a lemonade stand that gives characters extra lives.

SPORTS GAME SECRETS

Pro Evolution Soccer 6 allows gamers to turn their team into giant penguins or have their players ride ostriches or raptor dinosaurs. Midway's NBA Jam Tournament Edition contains an unusual Easter egg - secret codes call up an additional 40 characters to play games of basketball including the Beastie Boys band members, The Fresh Prince Will Smith, Prince Charles and former US president Bill Clinton!

PRANKS AND JOKES

Many Easter eggs are little in-jokes. In the jet ski racing game Wave Race: Blue Storm, a series of codes can change the commentary from enthusiastic and encouraging to sarcastic and rude! However, sometimes pranks backfire. Copies of Tiger Woods 99 PGA Tour Golf for PlayStation contained an entire unlicensed episode of South Park that one of the programming team had added for a joke. The game copies all had to be recalled.

Tiger Woods 99 PGA Tour Golf and Cartman from the TV show South Park.

An Easter egg in Tony Hawk Pro Skater 2 allows you to play as Spiderman.

MOST SECRET EASTER EGG

No one can be certain, as there may be some still undiscovered, but one of the longest-hidden Easter eggs occurred in Final Fantasy IX. Repeatedly returning to where the Tantalus Theater Troupe hide out allows gamers to complete an entire mini-quest. This Easter egg wasn't widely discovered until 2013, 13 years after the game was first released.

Gaming Easter eggs also appear in the operating systems of different machines. In Apple computers running OS X, Tetris and Pong are hidden inside the Terminal application. Even owners of some Kindle ebook readers can enjoy a game of Minesweeper or GoMoKu if they press Home, then hold down the Alt, Shift and M keys.

FIFA

By January 2016, the FIFA 15 Ultimate Team player who had scored the most goals was not Cristiano Ronaldo or Lionel Messi, but Adrián Ramos of Borussia Dortmund with 10.78 million goals. Daniel Sturridge was second with 10.27 million.

With Germany crowned football world champions at the 2014 World Cup, it's fitting that the record holder for the biggest win in a FIFA football game is also German. Patrick Hadler recorded an incredible scoreline in a FIFA World Cup 2014 game – playing as Germany against the Cook Islands, Hadler won 321-0!

Tottenham striker Harry Kane lines up a shot. Patrick Hadler recommends shooting between 17-22m (55-72ft) from goal to maximize goal-scoring chances.

LONG RUNNER

FIFA is the longest-running football action game, kicking off in 1993 with the release of FIFA International Soccer by Electronic Arts. It was the first football game to be officially licensed by FIFA – the organization that runs world football. The first edition to feature female players was FIFA 16 with 12 national women's teams: Germany, USA, France, Sweden, England, Brazil, Canada, Australia, Spain, China, Italy and Mexico.

FIFA DATA

CREATORS	EA Sports
PUBLISHER	Electronic Arts
LAUNCH	1993
TYPE	Sports simulation
MAJOR PLATFORMS	Xbox, PlayStation, Windows, iOS, Android

The top-five rated players in FIFA 17 are: Cristiano Ronaldo (rating: 94), Lionel Messi (above, 93), Neymar (92), Luis Suárez (92) and Manuel Neuer (92).

FAST SELLER

When it launched in late 2016, FIFA 17 smashed sales records for the series. In the first week after its launch, 6.9 million copies were sold! In February 2017, Fred Bugmann from Brazil set a new record for the most goals scored by a goalkeeper in a FIFA 17 game, notching up 21.

LONGEST MARATHON

Arsenal fan Chris Cook played an incredible 120 back-to-back matches on FIFA 15 at the Loading Bar gaming café in London in 2014. His 48-hour, 49-minute and 41-second marathon beat the previous record of 48 hours and 5 minutes, set by two Canadian gamers, Jordan Bloeman and Scott Francis Winder, in 2012.

KINECT ADVENTURES!

Unveiled all the way back in 2005, the Xbox 360 has been a hit with gamers who like their graphics in high definition (HD) or who want to play with others over the Internet using Xbox Live. Its biggest-selling game is the multi-sport Kinect Adventures! which, as of the start of 2016, had sold over 24 million copies worldwide.

! PIN UPS

Kinect Adventures! features five mini-games. These include River Rush, where you control a white-water raft, and Space Pop, which involves popping bubbles in a zero-gravity room. The aim in all of the games is to perform well enough to pick up adventure pins. The total number collected will influence whether the gamer gets a bronze, silver, gold or platinum medal at the end.

! CRACKING STUFF

In the Kinect Adventures! game 20,000 Leaks, players finds themselves underwater in a see-through glass cube. They have to move their arms and legs to plug as many as five leaks caused by marine life such as sharks, fish and crabs making cracks in the glass.

KINECT ADVENTURES! DATA

CREATOR	Good Science Studio
PUBLISHER	Microsoft Game Studios
LAUNCH	2010
TYPE	Adventure and multi-sport
MAJOR PLATFORMS	Xbox 360 with Kinect

! LOOK, NO GAMEPADS

Kinect Adventures! players have to get used to having no game controller in their hands. In fact, their body is the game controller. Kinect is a motion-sensing peripheral which cleverly uses infrared beams, like those used by a TV remote, to map the playing area in front of the sensor. Cameras in the Kinect bar track a person's movements and convert them into game commands whilst microphones pick up voice instructions.

In 2015, Andrew Peter Mee got a perfect score in one Kinect Adventures! game – Rallyball Sure Shot. He scored 191 points.

! FASTEST-SELLING PERIPHERAL

Games may sell fast but peripherals tend to sell more slowly, so it was quite an achievement for Kinect to sell at such a fast rate after its launch in November 2010. An average of 133,333 Kinect peripherals were sold on each of the first 60 days following its launch.

! MORE KINECT FUN

There are over 130 games available for the Kinect motion sensor, including Kinect-ready versions of classics like Madden NFL and FIFA. There are also a number of movie tie-in games including Kung Fu Panda, Toy Story Mania and Kinect Star Wars.

SIZE MATTERS

Bigger doesn't always mean better, as a number of tiny games machines prove. In 2009, US inventor Mark Slevinsky built the smallest arcade game cabinet. It measured just 124mm tall, 52mm wide and 60mm deep (4.9 x 2 x 2.4in) – not much bigger than your mobile phone. Incredibly, even smaller machines have been produced since then.

ARCADE IN YOUR PALM

After successful crowdfunding on the Internet, the Tiny Arcade was launched in 2016. It's the world's smallest arcade gaming cabinet on sale, and measures just 75mm by 40mm by 32mm (3 x 1.6 x 1.3in). Packed inside are speakers, a rechargeable battery and a microSD slot to download a range of games.

The TinyScreen is a customizable 25.8mm by 25mm (1 x 0.9in) colour screen that can be used in robotics or turned into a smartwatch. Fitted with two incredibly tiny joysticks, it can also be turned into a seriously small handheld console, 68mm wide and just over 25mm tall (2.7 x 1in).

EVEN THE BIG GUYS GO SMALL

Nintendo's Game Boy Micro is the smallest handheld cartridge console from a big manufacturer. Measuring just 50 × 101 × 17.2mm (2 x 4 x 0.7in), it weighs 80g (2.8oz). To compare, Nintendo's PlayStation 3 weighs 62 times as much!

BYTE-SIZED GAMES

Games, like all computer programs, can be measured in terms of the amount of memory their lines of code take. Many of the latest games contain millions of lines of code taking up many gigabytes (GB) of memory space. In 2015, French programmer Olivier Poudade produced a mini Pac-Man game called Pac-Man 256 which only takes up 256 bytes. This is a quarter of a kilobyte (KB) and less than the memory required to hold two Twitter tweets!

BIGGEST GAMES MACHINE

In contrast to these tiny machines, Jason Camberis spent two years building the world's biggest arcade console. His ArcadeDeluxe machine measures 1.93m wide by 1.06m deep (6.3 x 3.5ft) and at 4.41m (14.5ft) in height it is so tall that gamers have to climb steps that pull out from the bottom of the machine to reach the controls!

The ArcadeDeluxe weighs around 540kg (1,190lb) and features giant, 8cm (3.1in) wide, red control buttons, two eight-way joysticks and a huge 40cm (15.7in) diameter trackball as the game controls. Inside the machine, a PC and 1,000GB disk drive contain more than 250 classic arcade games including Pac-Man, LEGO Star Wars and Tiger Woods PGA Tour.

GAME CONTROLLERS

The Nintendo Entertainment System (NES) controller fits snugly in your hand, but the supersized model created by Benjamin Allen and other students at the Delft University of Technology in 2012 is an absolute whopper. Their monster gamepad measures 3.66m long, 1.59m wide and 0.51m tall (12 x 5.2 x 1.7ft) - about 30 times the size of the original controller.

✚ GIANT GAMEPAD

The jumbo NES gamepad weighs a hefty 120.2kg (265lb) and took students five months to build. It is fully functioning, although you do need two or three gamers to press or jump onto the buttons! Because of its size, mechanical switches couldn't be used inside. Instead, when a button is pressed, it breaks a beam of light and a sensor sends a signal to the console.

COMPLEX CONTROLS

One of the most complex game controllers ever built was for Capcom's Steel Battalion game for Xbox. The controller featured 40 buttons, three foot pedals and two joysticks which gamers had to master in order to control their giant battling robot in the game.

MAD CATZ

Mad Catz's L.Y.N.X.9 is one of the most flexible and, at US$299, most expensive game controllers for tablets and smartphones around. It can fold up into your pocket, offers Bluetooth and voice searching using its microphone, and its buttons and triggers can all be adjusted and will last for at least one million operations.

THE EMPEROR OF CONTROLLERS

The ultimate gaming chair for the super-rich, the MWE Emperor 200 features three multi-touch screens, surround sound and its own climate controls, but it doesn't include a console in its price of US$49,150.

CARBON CONTROLLER

Launched in 2016, the US$299 ColorWare Elite Titan Controller is made from gold carbon-fibre material, meaning it is incredibly strong. The controller contains three sets of thumb joysticks and two directional pads.

GAME VOICES

All the voices of the characters in the games you enjoy have to be created and made believable by skilled voice actors. The actor who has performed in the most video games is Steven Jay Blum from California. By the spring of 2015, he had acted in a staggering 354 different games.

ONE OF MANY

Some of the characters Steven Jay Blum has played include Crash Bandicoot in Crash Nitro Kart, The Penguin in LEGO Batman 2: DC Superheroes, Ethan Hunt in Mission Impossible - Operation Surma, and Vincent Valentine in 2016's Final Fantasy XV. Steve also voiced Wolverine in three different games in 2013 alone: Marvel Heroes, Deadpool and LEGO Marvel Super Heroes.

HEROINE AND HERO

Dragon Ball is a popular Anime and series of more than 25 video games. The voice for Son Goku - the all-action, young male hero in the game - is provided by a Japanese grandmother, Masako Nozawa! At the time of Dragon Ball Xenoverse's release in 2015 Nozawa was 79. In the 2010 Xbox 360 game Dragon Ball: Raging Blast 2, she played ten characters including Son Goku, Vegito and Bardock.

SUPER VOICE

Charles Martinet is an actor who appeared in TV shows such as ER and NYPD Blue but he is most famous as the voice of Nintendo's Mario character. Martinet has voiced Mario since 1995 in over 90 games and also does the voices of his brother, Luigi, as well as Wario and Toadsworth on occasion.

Son Goku in Dragon Ball is voiced by Masako Nozawa.

FAMOUS FACE... AND VOICE

Many voice actors are only known to hardcore gamers, but some famous movie stars have voiced characters in games. Elijah Wood, who played Frodo Baggins in the Lord of the Rings movies, voiced him in the game too. He also played Spyro the dragon in The Legend of Spyro action-adventure game.

LOTS OF LINES

Like all actors, voice actors have to learn their lines. And there can be a lot of them in the game. Star Wars: The Old Republic, for example, has more than 200,000 lines of dialogue shared out between a cast of hundreds of voice actors. It is thought to be one of the biggest scripts ever in computer gaming.

SPORTING SUPER-GAMES

Sports simulations have been popular ever since gaming began. Some, such as PGA Tour or NHL, mimic the gameplay of the sport. Others, such as Football Manager, focus on the tactics and team selection, allowing you to manage a sports team to glory. American football game Madden NFL was first released in 1988 and the game appears annually.

CONSTANT COMMENTARY

Madden NFL is named after commentator and former Super Bowl-winning coach of the Oakland Raiders, John Madden. The game features over 90,000 lines of commentary, the most found in any sports simulation. Madden himself commentated on the game up until Madden NFL 2009.

Madden NFL 2017 was the USA's bestselling game in August 2016. The same year, EA Sports announced the Madden NFL 17 Championship Series, the winner of which will collect a cool US$1 million!

TEEING OFF

Hot on the heels of Madden NFL's popularity comes PGA Tour, which was first released in 1990 and is still going strong. 2015 was the first time since 1998 that the game has not featured Tiger Woods in the title and on its cover, as he was replaced by Northern Irish golfer Rory McIlroy.

Madden NFL contains large amounts of data including detailed ratings on over 40 different attributes of each of the NFL's 2,500-plus players.

Over 100 million copies of Madden NFL have been sold across 30 different platforms, from MS-DOS to Apple iOS, Android and Windows PCs.

PAY TO THE ORDER OF **WADE McGILBERRY** $1,000,000
ONE MILLION DOLLARS
2K SPORTS
DATE 2K10
001
MEMO **PERFECTION**

BEGINNER'S LUCK

A new Xbox game, Major League Baseball 2K10, offered one million US dollars if any player could pitch a perfect game when it was released in 2010. Wade McGilberry scooped the prize on the day of the game's release having first played the game just 90 minutes earlier.

FROM GAME TO REALITY

In 2012, after years of playing football management games such as Football Manager, 21-year-old Vugar Huseynzade was appointed reserve team manager of Azerbaijan's premier league football club FC Baku. He held the job for over two years!

EXTREME SPORTS

Activision's Tony Hawk's Pro Skater is the most popular extreme sports series of all time. Over 30 million copies of these realistic skateboarding games have been sold.

THE SIMS

Games designer Will Wright lost his house and many of his possessions in a fire in 1991. It prompted him to think about how to create a simulation game where you build up a home and a life. The eventual result, The Sims, was released in 2000 to great acclaim.

◆ CUSTOMIZE YOUR LIFE

Create-A-Sim allows you to customize your characters. In The Sims 4 the customization extends to different ear sizes, body weight, 13 different eye colours and 18 different skin tones; as well as the sort of person they are from hot-headed to ambitious or quiet and bookish. Once created, The Sims 4 throws typical life problems at the characters who can experience 31 different emotions from bored or tense to confident or energized.

The language in the Sims is known as Simlish. It uses bits of English, Ukrainian, French and Latin, but was inspired by Navajo code talkers – native Americans who spoke in code and served with US forces during World War II.

BUILD A CITY

Before The Sims, there was SimCity. Will Wright's original simulation creation, released in 1989, involves building up a city from scratch and running it well so that it will flourish. It proved popular with many gamers and was developed for more than 20 different platforms including Windows, Linux, Nintendo DS and more recently Android and iOS. SimCity 2000 had sold 4.23 million copies as of 2015.

The latest version of the SimCity game (2013) features cities in glorious 3D and multiplayer cooperation and competition.

The Sims is popular in many countries. In 2005, the French Post Office issued a postage stamp in honour of the game.

Les Sims — FRANCE — La Poste 2005 — 0,33 €

THE SIMS DATA

CREATORS	Will Wright, Maxis/ The Sims Studio
PUBLISHER	Electronic Arts
LAUNCH	2000
TYPE	Life simulation
MAJOR PLATFORMS	Microsoft Windows, Mac OS X, Android, iOS

VAMPIRES

Released as a new game pack for The Sims 4 in 2017, Vampires features a new game world called Forgotten Hollow as well as new skills and vampire-related objects to collect.

The Sims

Will Wright collects pieces of old Soviet Union spacecraft and uses them to build competitive Battlebot robots.

PAC-MAN

When Toru Iwatani and his team at NAMCO created Pac-Man, he didn't know he had a sure-fire hit on his hands. The first ever Pac-Man machine, at the time called Puck-Man, was installed in a Tokyo cinema in 1980. By 1987 it had sold 293,822 machines.

MEET MS PAC-MAN

Ms Pac-Man, with a bow in her hair and lipstick around her pellet munching-mouth, was released as an arcade game machine in 1982 by Bally/Midway and later by NAMCO. She is thought to be the first female playable character in a video game. The game also sold well, with more than 115,000 machines produced.

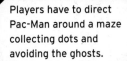

Players have to direct Pac-Man around a maze collecting dots and avoiding the ghosts.

PERFECT PAC-MAN

The highest score you can get on Pac-Man is 3,333,360 points. It requires lots and lots of work to gobble every single dot, ghost and bonus fruit found on all 256 game levels. In 1999, gaming legend Billy Mitchell from Hollywood, California became the first known player to rack up a perfect score – a task that took him over six hours.

PAC-MAN DATA

CREATOR	NAMCO
PUBLISHER	NAMCO and Bally/Midway
LAUNCH	1980
TYPE	Maze chasing
MAJOR PLATFORMS	Arcade, ported to various other systems

RACE-ING ALONG

In 2013, David Race from Ohio managed a perfect game in a record time of 3 hours, 28 minutes and 49 seconds. That's fast!

A boy dresses as Pac-Man at the 2015 Comic-Con International Convention.

BIGGEST HUMAN PAC-MAN

Pac-Man got a super-sized birthday memento in 2015 when 351 people formed the shape of a 10.5m (35ft) diameter Pac-Man in front of Japan's Tokyo Tower. Eleven years earlier, New York University students had re-enacted the game in real life, wearing costumes and chasing each other round 24 city blocks in the middle of New York. They called their game Pac-Manhattan!

GAME OVER

THE GHOSTS

In the American version of the game the four ghosts in Pac-Man have the nicknames of Inky, Blinky, Pinky and Clyde.

CHARACTER	/	NICKNAME
-SHADOW		"BLINKY"
-SPEEDY		"PINKY"
-BASHFUL		"INKY"
-POKEY		"CLYDE"

· 10 PTS

50 PTS

DAN'S THE MAN

In 2007, a Pac-Man World Championship was held in New York with ten top Pac-Man players competing against each other on a new version of the game, Pac-Man Championship Edition. The winner, Daniel Borrego from Mexico, received a new Xbox 360 console decorated with a Pac-Man design and signed by the game's originator, Toru Iwatani.

BESTSELLING SUPERHERO GAME

The bestselling superhero game isn't City of Heroes, The Amazing Spiderman or Marvel vs Capcom. The surprising fact is that the world's bestselling video game starring a superhero is part of the LEGO games franchise. LEGO Batman: The Videogame was released in 2008 and by the end of 2015 had sold a super-sized 13.2 million copies!

ACTION AND ADVENTURE

LEGO Batman is set in Gotham City and features a total of 30 official levels plus several 'secret' levels such as the Arkham Asylum. Gamers control one of many characters including superheroes and super villains such as the Penguin and the Joker, and use LEGO studs as currency throughout the game.

The soundtrack for the game is part of the movie score from the 1989 film Batman, directed by Tim Burton.

SEQUELS AND CINEMA

LEGO Batman proved so popular that two sequels have since been released - LEGO Batman 2: DC Super Heroes in 2012, and LEGO Batman 3: Beyond Gotham which features more than 150 playable characters. In 2017 LEGO Batman: The Movie releases, starring the voice talents of Oscar-nominated actor Ralph Fiennes, Michael Cera and singer Mariah Carey.

LEGO BATMAN: THE VIDEOGAME DATA

CREATOR	Traveller's Tales
PUBLISHER	Warner Bros Interactive Entertainment
LAUNCH	2008
TYPE	Action-adventure
MAJOR PLATFORMS	Xbox 360, PlayStation 2, PlayStation 3, PlayStation Portable, Nintendo DS, Microsoft Windows, Mac OS X, Wii

MAY THE FORCE BE WITH YOU

LEGO video games have been made celebrating Harry Potter, Star Wars, Indiana Jones and Pirates of the Caribbean. Together with the LEGO Batman series, these games have sold more than 100 million copies.

PREHISTORIC PLAYTIME

Released in 2015, LEGO Jurassic World allows gamers to adventure and solve puzzles inspired by the Jurassic Park movies. Players can even create their own terrifying dinosaurs.

Steve Blum, one of the world's top video game voice actors, was very busy on LEGO Batman. He performed the voices of Batman, the Joker and other characters in the game including Killer Moth, Killer Croc and Two-Face.

GUITAR HEROES

When it comes to serious riffs and solos on Guitar Hero, few can match Patrick Young. The man from Atlanta, Georgia undertook a truly epic music marathon in February 2012 and kept playing for an astonishing 72 hours, 17 minutes. Rock on... and on!

GUITAR HERO DATA

CREATOR	RedOctane and Harmonix
PUBLISHER	RedOctane, Activision
LAUNCH	2005
TYPE	Music rhythm game
MAJOR PLATFORMS	PlayStation, Xbox 360, Wii

ONE IN A MILLION

After working on Konami's Guitar Freaks arcade game, RedOctane began developing their own game in which users have to play the correct notes in sequence using a guitar-shaped controller. It cost US$1 million to launch the first Guitar Hero game in 2005 but it was worth it - the family of Guitar Hero games has made more than 2,000 times that sum.

GUITAR Hero

MOST NOTES IN A ROW

To gain high scores, Guitar Hero gamers have to hit as many of a song's notes as accurately as possible in the allocated time using their controller's buttons. In 2009, Danny Johnson from Texas took on Guitar Hero III's most difficult song, Through the Fire and Flames by heavy metal band DragonForce. He played all of the song's 3,722 notes in expert mode to notch up a record-breaking score of 973,954 points.

Danny Johnson also holds the record for the highest song score in the 2009 game Guitar Hero: Metallica – he played his way through an 11-minute song to score 1,009,056 points.

LIGHTNING LAUNCH

Guitar Hero III: Legends of Rock was the bestselling game of 2007 and the first music game to make over US$1 billion in sales. Activision sold a record 1.4 million copies in the first week alone!

MAKING A COMEBACK

In 2015, Guitar Hero made a comeback with Guitar Hero Live. Featuring a new, six-button guitar controller allowing more chords and hammer-ons, it gives gamers the chance to perform in front of a realistic live audience which gets more enthusiastic if you perform well, but jeers and heckles if you make lots of mistakes.

THE LEGEND OF ZELDA

The Legend of Zelda is a legendary game series. The original game can take 6-12 hours to complete but one gamer, known only as LackAttack24, became the first to complete a sub 30 minute speed run through the game in April 2015 - 29 minutes and 56 seconds to be precise.

FANTASY FUN

Zelda was the brainchild of Nintendo's Shigeru Miyamoto (who also helped create Mario, Super Mario and Donkey Kong). It is all about a silent, sword-wielding hero called Link who roams the strange, fantasy world of Hyrule performing quests and tasks which often involve rescuing Zelda and defeating the evil overlord, Ganon.

Link in The Legend of Zelda: Twilight Princess game.

ZELDA SALES DATA

OVER 75 MILLION COPIES OF ZELDA GAMES HAVE BEEN SOLD IN TOTAL. HERE ARE THE TOP FIVE BESTSELLERS SO FAR:

GAME	MILLIONS OF COPIES SOLD
Ocarina of Time	10.96
Twilight Princess	8.55
The Legend of Zelda	7.39
A Link To The Past	7.31
Link's Awakening	6.05

JOY FOR JOEL

Record breaker Joel Ekman works part-time as a curling instructor but streamed his speed runs of Zelda games on Twitch TV. In 2015, he recorded the first ever sub 18-minute time to complete Ocarina of Time – 17 minutes, 55 seconds – and was watched live by around 1,300 people.

THE STORY'S NOT OVER

Zelda is far from finished. Legend of Zelda: Breath of the Wild was released in March 2017 for the Wii U and the new Nintendo Switch console. Featuring a huge open game world 12 times larger than Zelda: Twilight Princess, the game sold more than 1.3 million copies in its first month.

One of the most highly-rated Zelda games, Ocarina Of Time, has a small programming bug which causes Link to run faster when going backwards rather than forwards!

THE LEGEND OF ZELDA DATA

CREATOR	Shigeru Miyamoto, Nintendo
PUBLISHER	Nintendo
LAUNCH	1986
TYPE	Action-adventure
MAJOR PLATFORMS	Gameboy, Wii, Nintendo DS, Nintendo 3DS, Wii U

MINECRAFT

With its open world and endless brick-building possibilities, Minecraft can be incredibly addictive. Ask the UK's Joseph Kelly, who in October 2015 notched up a marathon Minecraft session of 35 hours, 35 minutes and 35 seconds at a charity fundraising event!

BRICK-BUILDING BONANZA

With over 122 million copies sold, Minecraft is one of the world's most popular games. Its PC and Mac sales of 25.76 million by April 2017 make it the biggest-selling game for these machines ever. Minecraft is also the most-played game on Xbox Live, with two billion hours of playing time in its first two years on the platform.

This incredible winter palace is part of the huge Imperial City project. You can take a 3D tour on YouTube.

DANES IN THE GAME

An entire country has been recreated in Minecraft at 1:1 scale! The Danish Geodata Agency produced a map of over 42,000km² (16,220mi²) of Denmark, complete with buildings and landscape features. It took 4,000 billion bricks to produce the map, which needs an eye-boggling one terabyte (TB) of data storage.

MINECRAFT MEET

Minecraft's millions of fans converse on forums and messageboards but for face-to-face meetings, MINECON is the ultimate destination. On 24-25 September 2016, 12,000 fans from all over the world met at MINECON in Anaheim, USA – the biggest ever convention for a single game.

MINECRAFT DATA

CREATOR	Markus 'Notch' Persson
PUBLISHER	Mojang
LAUNCH	2009
TYPE	Sandbox, survival
MAJOR PLATFORMS	Xbox, PlayStation, Windows, Linux, iOS, Android

Beware Creepers in Minecraft. These mean green monsters can blow up a player's character if they get too close.

TESTING, TESTING

The first version of Minecraft was programmed in just six days and was initially called Cave Game. The game was perfected over the next two years, during which time more than 10 million users registered to play – the most players of a game during beta testing, ever.

SPACE GAME

In 1993, Russian astronaut Aleksandr A. Serebrov blasted off on a Soyuz TM-17 launch vehicle. The spacecraft docked with the MIR Space Station and Serebrov spent 196 days in space. He packed a Nintendo Game Boy along with a cartridge featuring the falling blocks puzzle game, Tetris, which became the first game to be played in space.

On its return to Earth, Serebrov's Game Boy and Tetris cartridge were auctioned at Sotheby's in London for US$1,220.

POCKET PLAY

The Game Boy was the fastest-selling console of its time when released in Japan in 1989. The first batch of 300,000 consoles was sold in just two weeks and in total 118.69 million Game Boys and Game Boy Colours were sold. It is second only to Nintendo DS as the most popular portable games machine of all time.

The original Game Boy required four AA batteries, had no backlight and could show just four different shades of grey on its screen. The console had just 8 KB of memory – a 32 GB smartphone today has four million times that!

GAME BOY COLOR

Nintendo

GAME BOY, GAME GIRL

The Game Boy originally came with a Tetris cartridge and options to buy Super Mario Land and four other games. The number of games available boomed to over 800, including The Legend of Zelda: Link's Awakening, Mega Man and Kirby's Dream Land. Until the Game Boy's release, gaming had been mostly for boys but in 1995 Nintendo America announced that 46% of all Game Boy players were girls.

The world's smallest digital camera when it debuted in 1999, Nintendo's Game Boy Camera took tiny pictures measuring just 256x224 pixels.

PLAY IT LOUD

Game Boys were later produced with lots of different case designs. These included the Play It Loud series of consoles which featured Game Boys in red, yellow, green and a super-cool clear casing letting you see all the console's components inside.

PLENTY OF PLAYERS

Before multi-player gaming began over the Internet, the first handheld game for more than four players was released in 1991 for the Game Boy. Faceball 2000 could be played simultaneously by up to 16 players, each of whom needed a console, a game cartridge, a connecting lead and adaptor. It all added up to a huge tangle of cables!

POKÉMON GO

Released in July 2016, Pokémon GO caused a sensation. The game was downloaded a record 130 million times within the first month after its launch. At one point, it was top of the charts of downloaded mobile games in 55 different countries at the same time!

Murkrow   Furret   Croconaw   Steelix   Wooper

In February 2017, over 80 new Pokémon were added to the game for players to seek out and capture. These included Murkrow, Furret, Croconaw, Steelix and Wooper.

When your trainer avatar is surrounded by a pink circle, you are within range of a Pokéstop.

CATCHING POKÉMON

There were originally just over 140 Pokémon for players to collect, from Geodude and Bulbasaur to Pidgey and Snorlax. In July 2016, New Yorker Nick Johnson was the first gamer to fill his Pokédex by collecting all 142 Pokémon available in the USA at the time. He walked over 153km to achieve his feat.

Lucky Egg   Revive   Razz Berry

POKÉSTOPS

In Pokémon GO, players roam their local area on the lookout for Pokémon as well as PokéStops. These handy places allow trainers to pick up useful items. Above Level 5, these include Revive potions as well as Razz Berries and Lucky Eggs.

Team Valor

Team Mystic

Team Instinct

⊕ IN THE GYM

Gyms are where trainers train their Pokémon and engage in combat. To join a gym, trainers have to ally themselves with one of the game's three teams: Valor (red), Mystic (blue) or Instinct (yellow).

Squirtle   Wartortle   Blastoise

⊕ EVOLVING POKÉMON

One of the game's addictive features is the ability to evolve lesser Pokémon into stronger types. For instance, the humble Magikarp water-type Pokémon can be evolved into the powerful dragon-like Gyarados, while a Squirtle can be evolved into a Wartortle which can then be transformed into a Blastoise.

⊕ POKÉMON GO GATHERING

The biggest meet up of Pokémon GO fans occurred in July 2016 when more than 5,000 game fans met up in Puerta del Sol public square in Madrid, Spain. The square contained two Pokémon gyms where gamers could train their Pokémon and fight other players' characters.

TETRIS

Games are often developed for one platform and then, if successful, the game is ported – converted so that it can run on other consoles and devices. The most ported game of all time, Tetris, began life in Russia in 1984. More than 210 versions of the official game have now been produced on over 60 platforms along with dozens more unofficial versions.

AWESOME ALEXEY

Alexey Pajitnov worked for the Soviet Academy of Sciences as a computer programmer when he developed a puzzle game featuring seven different designs of falling shapes, each made up of four blocks known as tetrominoes. Pajitnov named the game Tetris from the Greek word for four, 'tetra', combined with 'tennis' – his favourite sport.

SPREADING THE WORD

Tetris was written on a Soviet Electronika 60 computer and its first porting was to the IBM PC, followed by Commodore 64 and Amiga and Atari ST machines. Tetris has since appeared on almost every gaming console and personal computer and even on pocket calculators. The game also appears as an Easter egg on the HP54600B scientific oscilloscope used to analyze electronic signals.

TETRIS DATA

CREATOR	Alexey Pajitnov
PUBLISHER	Various
LAUNCH	1984
TYPE	Puzzle
MAJOR PLATFORMS	Multiple

TETRIS FOR GAME BOY

Thirty-five million copies of Tetris for the Game Boy have been sold since 1989. One of the key founders of the Apple computer company, Steve Wozniak, is a big Tetris fan and has the fourth-highest score ever achieved on the Game Boy version of the game – 507,110 points. The record score on the Game Boy was set by Uli Horner, in 2011, at 748,757 points.

RECORD YEARS

In 2015, a year after its 30th birthday, Tetris downloads to mobile devices passed the 500-million mark. In December 2016, Isaiah 'Triforce' Johnson set a world record for the most wins in 24 hours against the computer opponent Tetribot, in Tetris Ultimate (right). Johnson managed 614 victories during his epic gaming marathon.

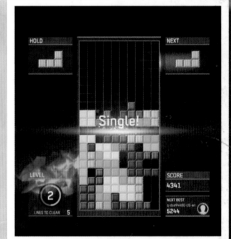

TOWERING TETRIS

Several giant versions of Tetris have been produced on the sides of buildings. In 2014, the world's biggest Tetris game was played on the side of the 29-floor, 133m (436ft) high Cira Centre in Philadelphia using hundreds of LED lights fitted into the glass of the building. Sega's Tetris Giant is the largest arcade version of Tetris. It stands over 2.2m (7.2ft) high and has joysticks with handles the size of basketballs.

GAME ADVERTISING

$

An estimated 113 million people tuned in to watch American football's Super Bowl in 2015. One of the adverts in the breaks starred actor Liam Neeson and was for the mobile strategy game Clash of Clans. By April 2017, the advert had received an incredible 159,188,760 views.

$ CLAN-TASTIC!

In Clash of Clans, you develop your own village, train your troops, mine for gold and seek magical liquid elixir and gems. You can gang up with others to defend your own village or attack others and be a part of a multi-player clan war.

There are different tiers, or levels, of troops in the game. The cheapest to obtain and the easiest to train are tier one troops such as archers and goblins.

$ MOBILE MONEY MAKER

Clash of Clans was developed by Supercell, a company from Finland. It is a freemium game which means it is free to download and play but gamers must pay for added features or to unlock new characters. According to SuperData Research, a massive US$1,345 million was spent on the game in 2015. That's a lot of wizards, archers and elixir!

CLASH OF CLANS DATA

CREATOR	Supercell
PUBLISHER	Supercell
LAUNCH	2012
TYPE	Multiplayer strategy
MAJOR PLATFORMS	Apple iOS, Android

$ GENIUS JORGE

With over 20 million active users, battling and sneaking your way to the top of the pile in Clash of Clans even for half a day is an almost impossible task. But a man from San Francisco, Jorge Yao, spent six months at the very top of the Clash of Clans leaderboard from January 2013. Yao became a gaming celebrity with 192,000 followers on Twitter by April 2017!

$ NAME A CHARACTER CONTEST

P.E.K.K.A are among the toughest armour-clad warriors in Clash of Clans. Back in 2012, Supercell organized a contest on Facebook for the best name that worked with those letters. The winning suggestion from a gamer called Victor was: 'Perfect Enraged Knight Killer of Assassins'.

The most powerful of all characters in the game are Heroes such as the Barbarian King and the Archer Queen, who wields a powerful crossbow.

FINAL FANTASY SOUNDTRACKS

No game series has spawned as many soundtracks as the epic Japanese role-play game series, Final Fantasy. There have been a total of 173 official soundtrack albums, the bestselling of which was Final Fantasy VIII, which sold around 300,000 copies in Japan.

♪ FIRST OF MANY

Hironobu Sakaguchi dropped out of university to start working at Japanese game makers, Square (now Square Enix) in 1983. Having suffered several flops in a row, the company was struggling and Sakaguchi assumed that his new game Fighting Fantasy would be his last, so renamed it Final Fantasy. It was anything but final, as the game proved a success and spawned 14 direct sequels.

♪ BIGGEST SELLER

Final Fantasy VII is the bestselling game in the series with over 9.72 million copies sold. It took around 120 people to develop it, whereas the original Final Fantasy required less than 10. The latest game in the series, Final Fantasy XV (right), was released in November 2016 and had sold an incredible six million copies by January 2017.

PS4
DAY ONE EDITION
FINAL FANTASY XV
TEEN
SQUARE ENIX

FINAL FANTASY DATA

CREATOR	Hironobu Sakaguchi
PUBLISHER	Square Enix (formerly SquareSoft)
LAUNCH	1987
TYPE	Role-playing game
MAJOR PLATFORMS	PS2, PS3, PS4, Xbox One, Xbox 360, Wii, Windows, Nintendo 3DS, Android, iOS

Gilgamesh has been a popular character since Final Fantasy V. This eight-armed battle boss is frequently dressed in brightly coloured armour.

♪ COMMON CHARACTERS

Final Fantasy includes a number of reoccurring characters including Barrett, Gilgamesh, Wedge and Biggs. There are also common creatures such as Chocobos, which are usually large, flightless birds, giant armoured turtle-like beasts called Adamantoise, and Moogles, which have distinctive red wings.

More Friends: Music From Final Fantasy was a live recording held at the Universal Amphitheatre, Los Angeles in May 2005 and featured the World Festival Symphony Orchestra conducted by Arnie Roth. The album was released the following year.

♪ EAT IT UP

Final Fantasy continues to be of great appeal to gamers, especially in Japan where in 2014, a diner dedicated to the games opened in Tokyo. Named the Eorzea Café after the region of Eorzea which was the setting for Final Fantasy XIV, the café is decorated in the style of the games and contains computers so that visitors can play as they eat and drink.

POKÉMON

The handheld Nintendo 3DS is popular with gamers on the go and many of its games have sold in their millions – none more so than the reboot of the famed Pokémon series. Over 1.2 million people in Japan pre-ordered Pokémon X and Pokémon Y before they were released in October 2013. By the start of 2017 the games had sold a record 16.06 million copies.

OTHER BESTSELLING 3DS GAMES

MARIO KART 7	14.82 million
POKÉMON SUN/ POKÉMON MOON	14.69 million
POKÉMON OMEGA RUBY/ POKÉMON ALPHA SAPPHIRE	13.68 million
SUPER MARIO 3D LAND	11.17 million
NEW SUPER MARIO BROS. 2	11.09 million

BATTLING IN KALOS

Pokémon X and Y are based in the Kalos region where gamers must train and battle to obtain the eight gym badges of Kalos. Using the Nintendo 3DS's graphic abilities, Pokémon X and Y are the first Pokémon games in full 3D and feature a Player Search System. When linked to the Internet, gamers can keep track of others playing the game, allowing them to attempt trades or battles.

BIG BEAST COLLECTION

Gamers begin with one of three starter Pokémon: Chespin, Fennekin or Froakie. These three Pokémon grow and evolve the more they battle and the more the game is played. Including new fairy-type characters, Pokémon X and Y games have a total of 719 different Pokémon – the biggest collection of any game.

The Nintendo 3DS was the first handheld console to give gamers 3D graphics without needing to wear glasses. It also features StreetPass - a feature which signals when other 3DS owners are nearby and allows players to share information and play certain games with each other.

Pokémon X and Y are the first games to feature mega evolution where a Pokémon can evolve past its previous limits, but only during battle.

A soundtrack album from the games was released in 2013 and reached number 12 in the Billboard Japan music charts.

POKÉMON X AND POKÉMON Y DATA

CREATOR	Game Freak
PUBLISHER	The Pokémon Company
LAUNCH	2013
TYPE	Role-playing game
MAJOR PLATFORMS	Nintendo 3DS

Starter Pokémon Chespin

STAR CHARACTER

It took a lot of gaming and a lot of counting but one character has appeared in more games than any other in the history of video gaming. Mario, the brightly coloured little plumber with a moustache, has starred in over 220 video games!

★ THE LEGEND BEGINS

Mario first appeared as the character Jumpman in Nintendo's 1981 arcade game Donkey Kong. The brains behind the game, Shigeru Miyamoto, had tried but failed to get the rights to make a video game based on cartoon character Popeye, so he made Donkey Kong instead, with Mario in the hero role.

★ MILLIONS OF MARIOS

The Super Mario World series, including Super Mario Galaxy, Super Mario 3D World and many others, is the bestselling game series in the world. By the end of 2015, it had sold a mindboggling 311.46 million copies. Add in over 110 million sales for Mario Kart, 40 million for Mario Party and more for other games besides and you get a grand total of more than 530 million.

1985's landmark game Super Mario Bros has sold 40.24 million copies – the bestselling Mario game ever!

MARIO KART 8

The latest Mario Kart racing game has lots of different circuits you can compete on. In March 2017, a French gamer called Victor posted a record time for a lap around the Mario Kart Stadium circuit of 1 minute, 34.144 seconds. The next month, a Canadian gamer called Sgt Guy posted the fastest-ever time around the Bowser's Castle circuit of 1 minute, 58.18 seconds.

Mario first got a taller brother, Luigi, in the 1983 game Mario Bros. They were both cast as plumbers.

GAME AWARDS

The Golden Joystick Awards are the longest-running video game awards with the first edition being held all the way back in 1983. In that year, Jetpac beat Manic Miner, The Hobbit adventure game and Arcadia to become the first ever winner of the Golden Joystick. The 2016 awards, held in London, UK, were the 34th edition.

🏆 FIRST PRIZE

Developed for the ZX Spectrum and later the VIC 20 and BBC Micro, Jetpac involved gamers controlling a character as it assembled a rocket to fly off to other planets.

🏆 DOUBLE WINNER

At the 2016 Golden Joystick Awards, Pokémon GO scooped the awards for both Innovation of the Year and the Handheld/Mobile Game of the Year.

SELECTED GAME OF THE YEAR WINNERS

1983	Jetpac
1984	Knight Lore
1985	Way of the Exploding Fist
1986	Gauntlet
1988/89	Operation Wolf
1990	The Untouchables
1992/93	Street Fighter II
1996/97	Super Mario
2004	Pro Evolution Soccer 4
2012	The Elder Scrolls V: Skyrim

LittleBIGPlanet won the Family Game of the Year award in 2009. In the same year the game won eight prizes at another awards ceremony held by the Academy of Interactive Arts & Sciences (AIAS).

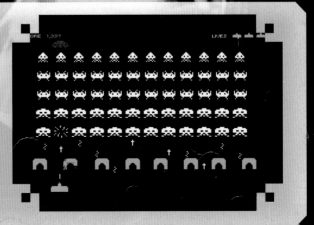

🏆 NINTENDO PRIZE

Nintendo games have their own awards category at the Golden Joysticks. The 2015 winner was the fun and chaotic paint-splattering shooter game Splatoon (above), which has sold over four million copies for the Wii U. The Legend of Zelda: Twilight Princess HD took the prize in 2016.

Kerbal Space Program won the Best Indie Game at the 2015 Golden Joystick Awards. The game features a race of small green creatures called the Kerbals, and involves designing, building and flying space planes and rockets to visit and explore 13 different planets and moons.

🏆 FIRST GAMES AWARDS

Organized by US magazine Electronic Games, the Arcade Awards (often known as the Arkie Awards) were the very first video game awards. They were first held in 1979 and ran until 1984. Space Invaders was the original Game of the Year winner, with Asteroids the winner in the arcade category and the best console game category the following year.

MORE ABOUT MINECRAFT

Minecraft is massive, there's no doubt about it. It's so influential that it was the most used search term on YouTube in 2014 and the world-famous British Museum in London has started a long-term project to model the entire museum and all its treasures in the game.

FIRST NATIONAL MINECRAFT CHAMPION

The Minecraft National Championship was first held in 2015 in the USA with challenges and competitions in 40 cities over six weeks. The winner and US champion was SuperKraft11 who turned out to be a ten-year-old boy from Los Angeles called Julien Wiltshire.

CREATIVE CONSTRUCTION

Millions of people love to build in Minecraft and some have been incredibly creative. Their constructions include a five-million block model of the Battlestar Galactica spaceship, entire worlds modelled on the Harry Potter or Lord of the Rings universes and even a 1.6km (1mi) long playable guitar built by committed Minecrafter FVDisco from Australia.

MOBS RULE!

Mobile creatures and monsters in Minecraft are known as mobs. The very first animal mobs were pigs in an August 2009 update to the game. In the same month came the first hostile mob – Zombies! They were quickly followed by skeletons who can fire arrows.

You can ride pigs in Minecraft if you can find a saddle in a chest in a dungeon. To control the pig well, though, you need to dangle a carrot from the end of a fishing rod in front of its snout!

LARGEST REAL COUNTRY MADE IN MINECRAFT

In 2013 the UK Ordnance Survey agency, which produces detailed maps, produced a model of almost all of Great Britain. The 224,000km^2 (86,500mi^2) area required a lot of work as it used an amazing 50,000 million Minecraft blocks!

The longest tunnel in Minecraft was created by gamer ItzEpicGeorge, and by 2017 it measured 100,000 blocks long. That's equal to 100km or twice the distance between the English cities of Manchester and Liverpool.

FIRST MINECRAFT GAME ON WII U

Minecraft: Story Mode, created by Telltale Games, was released for most platforms in October 2015. It features a new character, Jesse, who must find allies to help save the gameworld from the Witherstorm. In December 2015 it became the first Minecraft game to be released for the Nintendo Wii U.

ANGRY BIRDS

Formed by three students in 2003, Rovio is a Finnish games company that had a minor hit with the multiplayer game King of the Cabbage World. It was largely unknown until it released its 52nd game in 2010. Angry Birds and its sequels have since become the most downloaded mobile game series of all time, with more than two billion downloads.

FEATHERED FRIENDS

The game is set on Piggy Island where pigs have been stealing birds' eggs - but the birds are now fighting back. Gamers have to sling the birds at the pesky pigs and solve puzzles to attack. Different birds have different attributes - for instance, hefty Terence can smash his way through any defence and Stella can blow big soap bubbles to trap objects inside.

PESKY PIGS

So many gamers liked the pigs even though they were the villains that Rovio produced a spin-off game, Bad Piggies. When released in September 2012, it became the fastest game to reach number one in Apple's App Store, taking just three hours!

ANGRY BIRDS DATA

CREATOR	Rovio
PUBLISHER	Rovio
LAUNCH	2009
TYPE	Puzzle
MAJOR PLATFORMS	Android, iOS, Windows Phone, Windows, OS X

Rovio's official spokesperson, Peter Vesterbacka, has an unusual job title – 'Mighty Eagle'!

SEQUEL SUPER SCORES

Released in 2012, Angry Birds Star Wars mixes Angry Birds mayhem with the Star Wars characters and settings. In the Android version of the game, on Level 1 of Tattooine, Marc Cohen holds the record high score of 45,280 points. Also in 2015, Andrew Mee obtained the first perfect score on Angry Birds Rio – Smugglers Den with 48,180 points.

WINGING IT

Angry Birds has inspired a TV cartoon series called Angry Birds Toons, a movie, and even three official theme parks in the UK, Finland and Malaysia.

WHAT'S IN STORE?

The first official Angry Birds store opened in Helsinki, Finland in 2013. It sells clothes, plush toys, bags, books and accessories all branded with Angry Birds characters. Other Angry Birds products include shampoo, soft drinks and potato chips!

CANDY CRUSH SAGA

The world of gaming on Facebook is constantly changing. Several games have vied for the title of most popular Facebook game, including FarmVille 2, but Candy Crush Saga swept away all before it after its release in April 2012. In the month of November 2015 the game was played by 149.57 million active players!

 BIG MONEY

Candy Crush Saga was released for smartphones at the end of 2012 and later for Windows 10. All versions of the game are free to play but players can buy extra lives and tools to help complete certain tough levels and to unlock new levels. According to gaming statisticians Think Gaming, in April 2017 gamers were spending around US$1.4 million on the game each day!

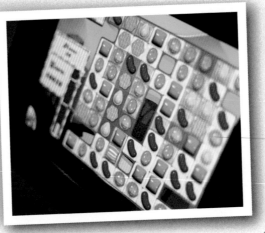

MEGA LEVELS

Candy Crush Saga's makers, King Games, have repeatedly added new levels to the game for players to test out. By April 2017 there were thought to be a staggering 3,115 levels available.

SWEET SEQUELS

A sequel called Candy Crush Soda Saga was launched in 2014, and as of 2017 it has more than 1,400 levels. In 2016 Candy Crush Jelly Saga became the second sequel. It features marshmallow characters called pufflers and a boss mode where gamers have to battle a computer opponent in Candy Kingdom - the Jelly Queen.

ON THE FARM

Farming simulation game FarmVille was launched in 2009 and for two years was Facebook's most popular game. FarmVille 2 followed in 2012 and it too became highly popular with 40 million monthly active users in 2013.

Candy Crush Saga's Facebook page had notched up over 74.49 million 'Likes' by April 2017, making it the most liked game on the social network.

CANDY CRUSH SAGA DATA

CREATOR	King Digital Entertainment
PUBLISHER	King Digital Entertainment
LAUNCH	2012
TYPE	Puzzle game
MAJOR PLATFORMS	Facebook, iOS, Android, Windows Phone, Windows 10

Appetizing and addictive, by January 2014 gamers had already played over 150 billion games of Candy Crush Saga.

MMORPGs

Massively Multiplayer Online Role-Playing Games (MMORPGs) take place in a large world with thousands, or sometimes millions, of players. Characters can often form alliances with others and seek a profession or quests and adventures to go on. Star Wars: The Old Republic was launched in 2011 and gained over a million subscribers within three days of its launch – making it the fastest-growing MMORPG ever!

GAME EMPIRE

Created by Bioware and rumoured to have cost more than US$200 million to make, Star Wars: The Old Republic allows players to join as members of either the Galactic Republic or the Sith Empire. The game has been extended with six expansion packs, the latest being Knights of the Eternal Throne in December 2016, which added new characters and worlds to explore.

LONGEST RUNNING

Whilst The Realm, which began in 1996, is considered the longest-running multiplayer online game, its users today only number in the hundreds. Ultima Online, which was released in 1997, by contrast, became the first MMORPG to gain 100,000 players and is still going strong today with a new expansion pack, Time of Legends, released in 2015.

EXPENSIVE PROPERTY

Certain MMORPGs allow gamers to buy in-game possessions and property. The most expensive piece of property bought so far in a MMORPG was the Crystal Palace Space Station in the game Planet Calypso. In January 2010, Canadian Erik Novak bought the space station for an out-of-this-world US$330,000.

MMORPG ON A MOBILE

The first MMORPG for mobile phones was Shade, released in August 2003. Written by Canadian David Dies and published by Cosmic Infinity, some 30,000 players joined up and amassed 18 million minutes of gameplay within its first year.

Final Fantasy XI, released in 2002, was the first MMORPG to allow gamers to play each other using different console platforms including PC, PlayStation 2 and Xbox 360.

Eve Online is a MMORPG set in space where gamers can customize their spaceships to explore 7,800 worlds. It gained 500,000 subscribers by 2014.

WORLD OF WARCRAFT

Welcome to Azeroth! MMORPGs are big but the biggest of all is World of Warcraft (WoW). By 2012 this massive game had attracted a peak of 12 million active subscribers and by 2014 had brought in over US$10 billion in revenue!

WORTH THE WAIT

World of Warcraft developed out of earlier Warcraft games including Warcraft III: Reign of Chaos. These earlier games were single or multiplayer games but WoW was designed on a far grander scale. It took 150 developers more than four years to build the game's 1,400 locations. The final game was made up of 5.5 million lines of computer program code.

MOST SUBSCRIPTIONS

A record total of over 100 million separate accounts have been created by gamers keen on entering the mystical world of Azeroth. World of Warcraft also holds the record for the number of characters created, over 500 million as of 2015.

Only 1% of all WoW players choose to be neutral. The other 99% either join the Alliance or the Hoard.

WORLD OF WARCRAFT DATA

CREATOR	Blizzard Entertainment
PUBLISHER	Blizzard Entertainment
LAUNCH	2004-05 (dependent on region)
TYPE	MMORPG
MAJOR PLATFORMS	Microsoft Windows, Apple OS X

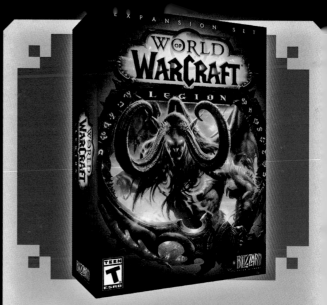

It would take 44 CDs to store all the 3,900 minutes of music and sound effects found in World of Warcraft.

🔨 WORD UP

Released in 2016, Legion was the sixth WoW expansion pack. These have expanded the amount of text in the game to a staggering six million words – that's more than 13 times the number of words in the Lord of The Rings trilogy and 31 times more than *Harry Potter and The Goblet of Fire*. Even the game's Wikia site is record-breaking as it contains over 103,000 pages, the biggest for any game in the world.

A Junglebeak character from World of Warcraft.

🔨 MOST COLLECTABLE PETS

There are a record 619 collectable pets in World of Warcraft from Amerbarb wasps and Biletoads to Hawk owls, bear cubs and even clockwork gnomes! The most popular pet for players is a squirrel.

🔨 QUEST SUCCESS

One anonymous gamer, or it might be a group of gamers under one name, became the first to complete all 986 achievements in WoW by 2009. 'Little Gray' from Taiwan completed 5,906 quests and defeated 380,895 creatures on the path to glory.

STREET FIGHTER

In 2010, in the space of four hours, Ryan Hart took on and beat 169 Street Fighter IV challengers. His record-breaking winning streak set in Hull, England, saw him play each game as Sagat, the muay thai specialist.

In 2016, Ryan Hart defeated 260 opponents in a row in a marathon 11-hour session of Street Fighter V held at the Trafford Centre in Manchester, UK.

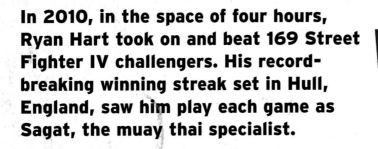

FIGHTING STREET ™

SELECT AND PUSH RUN BUTTON
▶   ONE PLAYER
        OR
    PLAYER1 VS PLAYER2
Ⓒ 1989 HUDSON SOFT;
Ⓒ 1987 CAPCOM.   CREDIT 3

★ STILL PUNCHING

Street Fighter debuted in 1987 and is still going strong with a record 127 different games produced under the franchise. These include arcade favourites such as Street Fighter II, one of the first games to feature six buttons and an eight-way joystick to enable players to pull more than 30 moves. The hotly anticipated Street Fighter V was released for Windows and PlayStation 4 in August 2016.

STREET FIGHTER DATA

CREATORS	Hiroshi Matsumoto, Takashi Nishiyama
PUBLISHER	CAPCOM
LAUNCH	1987
TYPE	Fighting
MAJOR PLATFORMS	Arcades, Xbox, PlayStation, Windows, Linux, iOS, Android

A fan dresses like Chun-Li, who in the Street Fighter games is famous for her fast multiple attacks on opponents.

★ GIRL POWER!

Chun-Li became the first playable female character in a fighting game when she debuted in Street Fighter II in 1991. She has appeared in nearly every Street Fighter variant ever since. While playing the character of Chun-Li, France's Marie-Laure Norindr – known as 'Kayane' – became the first female gamer to become a professional Street Fighter champion when she triumphed at the 2010 Evolution Championship Series.

GRAN TURISMO

The long-running Gran Turismo series celebrated its 15th year in 2012 before debuting its latest game, Gran Turismo 6 (GT6) the following year. Gran Turismo 5 had been the first racing simulation to feature over 1,000 cars but GT6 overtook its predecessor boasting an incredible 1,237 different vehicles.

Ferrari Dino 246 GT

SUPER FLEET

Amongst the record-breaking fleet of cars gamers have to choose from are old-time classics such as the 1957 BMW 507, the 1971 Ferrari Dino 246 GT and the 1978 Pontiac Firebird Trans Am. These are mixed with the latest and greatest super sports cars including the SRT Viper GTS, the Aston Martin One-77 and leading NASCAR vehicles such as Chevrolet SS racers.

GRAN TURISMO 6 DATA

CREATOR	Team led by Kazunori Yamauchi
PUBLISHER	Sony Computer Entertainment
LAUNCH	2013
TYPE	Racing Simulation
MAJOR PLATFORMS	PlayStation 3

FUTURE RACING

For GT6 the game developers, Polyphony Digital, invited 22 car manufacturers, including Lexus, Mercedes-Benz and Aston Martin, to produce their own futuristic concept vehicles for inclusion in the game. Bugatti not only supplied a digital version of their super-fast Chiron Vision concept car, but they also built a full-size design in real life.

By 2017, 76.84 million copies of Gran Turismo games had been sold, making it the most successful car racing game of all time.

MOST CIRCUITS

With 86 circuits on its release, Gran Turismo 6 has the most tracks of any racing simulation game. A track editor allows gamers to create their own variations, and entirely new courses, leading to an infinite number of tracks to race on.

REAL-LIFE RACING

Racing nut Kazunori Yamauchi led a team of seven to design the first Gran Turismo game, which was released in 1997 after five years of hard work. Yamauchi actually races real-life Nissan GT-R cars, a vehicle for which he helped design the interactive dashboard display.

GAMERS GALORE

Held from October 2012 to May 2013, the 2013 FIFA Interactive World Cup drew a huge entry from gamers who play the FIFA game and were keen to take on the top players around the world. A world record 2,541,519 FIFA gamers took part. That's more than 34 times the number of fans sat in the Maracana Stadium in Brazil to watch the real 2014 FIFA World Cup final!

FIFA
1st Place
DIPLOMA
Bruce Grannec (FRA)

2013 champion Bruce Grannec likes to play as Real Madrid in FIFA.

PLAYER SIGNING

The beaten finalist of the 2014 tournament, David Bytheway from Wolverhampton, England, was signed in 2016 by real-life German football club VfL Wolfsburg to play FIFA in competitions wearing the German club's colours.

The FIFA Interactive World Cup was first held in 2004 at FIFA's headquarters in Switzerland and has been held every year since except 2007.

FIFA INTERACTIVE WORLD CUP HOSTS AND WINNERS

Year	Host	Winner (Nationality)
2004	Switzerland	Thiago Carrico de Azevedo (Brazil)
2005	England	Chris Bullard (England)
2006	Netherlands	Andries Smit (Netherlands)
2008	Germany	Alfonso Ramos (Spain)
2009	Spain	Bruce Grannec (France)
2010	Spain	Nenad Stojkovic (Serbia)
2011	USA	Francisco Cruz (Portugal)
2012	United Arab Emirates	Alfonso Ramos (Spain)
2013	Spain	Bruce Grannec (France)
2014	Brazil	August Rosenmeier (Denmark)
2015	Germany	Abdulaziz Alshehri (Saudi Arabia)
2016	USA	Mohamad Al-Bacha (Denmark)

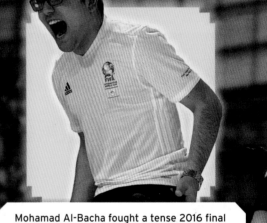

Mohamad Al-Bacha fought a tense 2016 final with England's Sean Allen. Al-Bacha won on away goals after the score was tied 5-5.

WORLD CUP FOR ALL

The competition was traditionally only available to players using PlayStations but the 2016 tournament was playable on both Xbox One and PS4. Around 2.3 million entrants battled it out to be one of the 32 elite players to compete in New York. The 2017 final will be hosted in London in August and promises a visit to a real-life football awards ceremony and a prize of US$200,000 to the winner.

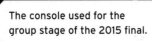

The console used for the group stage of the 2015 final.

SUPER MARIO RUN

When Nintendo announced the first ever Mario smartphone game, Super Mario Run, excitement began to build. There were a record 50 million downloads in the week after its launch on 15 December 2016, making it a record breaker as the fastest-selling app for Apple devices.

APPLE THEN ANDROID

Super Mario Run was first released exclusively for Apple devices and, despite being released in mid-December, it became the 10th most downloaded app from the Apple app store for the entire year! In March 2017, the game was released for Android smartphones and tablets.

SIDE SCROLLER

Super Mario Run is a side-scrolling platform game in which Mario runs through a series of screens and levels. Players tap the screen to make Mario jump - the longer they press the screen, the higher the character flies. Successful players can unlock characters such as Yoshi, Princess Peach and Luigi, and play as them instead of Mario.

TOAD RALLIES AND KINGDOM BUILDING

The Toad Rally mode of the game allows players to compete against ghost characters which have already completed the level. Performing well in a toad rally gains you toad followers and coins with which you can buy items such as houses, mushrooms and staircases. Use these to construct your own mushroom kingdom in Kingdom Builder mode.

There are five rainbow bridges to unlock, allowing players to extend their kingdom until it's made up of six different areas.

MEET THE TEAM

The game was designed by Takashi Tezuka while Nintendo legend Shigeru Miyamoto (above) was the game's producer. It was the first time in a decade that Miyamoto, who designed games including Super Mario Bros and Legend of Zelda, had been so closely involved with a game's creation.

LIVE AUDIENCES

The world of eSports has grown and grown and that includes the numbers of fans keen to watch the top gamers perform. Tournaments are particularly popular in South Korea – in 2005, an estimated 120,000 fans flocked to Gwangalli Beach in Busan to watch the final of the SKY Proleague tournament where teams battled it out playing StarCraft.

STARCRAFT FANS

StarCraft is a real-time strategy game set in space. Released in 1998, the game sold almost ten million copies worldwide over the next decade. Half of these were bought by South Korean gamers and major eSports leagues and tournaments grew up in South Korea around the game and its sequel, StarCraft II: Wings of Liberty. Champion players like Choi Yeon-sung and Lim Yo-hwan became national celebrities.

An expansion pack for StarCraft II.

A member of the Jin Air Green Wings team competes in the StarCraft II 2015 tournament.

TEAM SPIRIT

The South Korean Air Force founded their own StarCraft gaming team, The Ace Team, in 2007 to allow top Korean StarCraft players to still compete when performing their compulsory two years of military service. The professional team Jin Air Green Wings has a major sponsor in the form of Jin Air, part of Korean Airlines.

In total, eSports fans watched 386 million hours worth of action from the 2015 League of Legends Championship.

According to the eSports Conference, 256 million people around the world watched eSports competitions in 2016.

SK Telecom T1 won the title in 2016, becoming the first three-time winners of the championship.

ONLINE AUDIENCES

The 2016 League of Legends Championship final saw 20,000 people flock to the Staples Centre in Los Angeles, USA to watch the action live as teams battled it out for a prize pool worth US$6.7 million. A further 43 million people followed the final online, setting a world record for eSports viewing and beating the 2015 edition, which drew an online audience of around 37 million people.

PLAY TO WIN BIG

There's some big money to be won in professional gaming competitions, particularly in The International for DotA 2. The competition boasted total prize winnings of 1.6 million US dollars in 2011, with a cool million going to winning team Natus Vincere. By 2015 the prize pot had soared to US$18,429,613!

⭐ STANDALONE SEQUEL

Defense of the Ancients (DotA) was built as a modification to the game Warcraft III: Reign of Chaos and allowed players to battle each other. It proved so popular that a sequel, DotA 2, was developed and launched in 2013. It is a complete standalone game, free to play online and features teams of five who must destroy their opponents' structure called the Ancient.

Each player controls one of 111 different types of character known as Heroes. These include the popular Rubick (above) the Grand Magus, the powerful Earthshaker and the razor-sharp goblin Timbersaw.

⭐ SPECTATOR SPORT

Sixteen teams took part in the 2015 Internat tournament for DotA 2, which was held at th KeyArena in the US city of Seattle. It took ju ten minutes for all 10,000 spectator tickets t be sold after they were announced. Hundred thousands more followed the tournament or via live streams or, if they were DotA 2 playe from within the game itself.

DEFENSE OF THE ANCIENTS 2 DATA

CREATOR	IceFrog & Valve Corporation
PUBLISHER	Valve Corporation
LAUNCH	2013
TYPE	Multi-player online battle game
MAJOR PLATFORMS	Windows, OS X, Linux

⊞ WINGS WIN

The International 2016 edition saw the Digital Chaos team reach the final and claim a prize of US$3,427,126 as runners-up. They were defeated by Chinese team Wings Gaming (above), who scooped an eyepopping US$9,139,002 – the biggest single prize won by an eSports team at one tournament.

⊞ YOUNGEST CHAMPION

One member of the triumphant Evil Geniuses team was Sumail Hassan Syed, known as SumaiL. Hailing from Pakistan, he was just 16 years and 82 days old when he won The International in 2015. This made him the youngest known champion and the youngest to win a million dollars at a single tournament.

In April 2014, just over 7.86 million gamers played DotA 2. By 2017, the number of players in the month of March alone was 12,658,054!

POKÉMON CHAMPIONSHIPS

The Pokémon World Championships have been held since 2002 for trading cards and since 2009 for video games. In 2010 Ray Rizzo, originally from New Jersey, won the Senior Division of the 2010 World Championships. He followed it up with two further victories in 2011 and 2012 to become the first three-time Pokémon world champion.

🏆 A FIRST FOR KOREA

In 2014, after many years of American or Japanese domination, Se Jun Park defeated Jeudy Azzarelli in the final held in Washington D.C. to become the first Pokémon World Champion from South Korea. One of his key Pokémon was Pachirisu, a squirrel-like creature that charges electricity in its cheek pouches and can give opponents electric shocks.

🏆 BIGGEST POKÉMON PRIZE POOL

Shoma Homami from Japan was crowned 2015 Pokémon World Champion. This tournament was held in the American city of Boston and featured the biggest prize pot so far, with US$2 million worth of cash and scholarships on offer.

Ray Rizzo (below) beat Japan's Jumpei Yamamoto and two fellow Americans, Joe Pulkowski and Wolfe Glick, to be crowned champion in 2012. Glick won the 2016 title as part of an American clean sweep, with Carson Confer winning the Senior Division and Cory Connor winning the Junior Division.

🏆 PLENTY OF PLAYERS

The Pokémon Red game holds the record for the most players taking part in an online single-player game. In 2014, Twitch TV organized a Twitch Plays Pokémon event in which 1,165,140 gamers took part.

🏆 POKÉPARK

In 2005 a dedicated theme park for Pokémon opened in the Japanese city of Nagoya. Nicknamed PokéPark, it ran from March to September and then opened up in Taiwan the following year.

CHAMPIONSHIP GAMES

MOST YEARS, A DIFFERENT POKÉMON GAME HAS BEEN USED BY PLAYERS COMPETING AT THE WORLD CHAMPIONSHIPS.

2009 Pokémon Platinum
2010 Pokémon HeartGold and SoulSilver
2011 Pokémon Black and White
2012 Pokémon Black and White
2013 Pokémon Black 2 and White 2
2014 Pokémon X and Y
2015 Pokémon Omega Ruby and Alpha Sapphire
2016 Pokémon Omega Ruby and Alpha Sapphire

Glenn and Linda Arnold and their three children Ryan, David and Grace all play Pokémon competitively. The family of five from the US state of Illinois have each qualified for the Pokémon World Championships!

CROWDFUNDED GAMES

Crowdfunding is when games-makers or inventors go online to raise funds by getting large numbers of people to contribute small amounts. In 2012, Chris Roberts started raising funds for a massive space game set in the 30th century called Star Citizen. The initial fundraising target was rapidly reached and by March 2017 the game had raised a mind-boggling US$146,446,483!

SPACED OUT

Star Citizen mixes exploration, space trading and spaceship dogfights in a giant fictional universe of inhabited planets, stars and alien races. The game will feature unlimited gameplay with vast numbers of gamers roaming its universe of stunning graphics.

CITIZENS OF THE STARS

People who have signed up to help the game develop are known as Star Citizens. By April 2017, there were a record 1,778,921 star citizens. In return for their aid, Star Citizens get early access to the game's different modules, game credits and currency. They also get their own spaceship and a hangar in the game to store it in!

MOST CROWDFUNDED CONSOLE

The Ouya was a small, affordable Android games console developed by Ouya Inc. In 2012, they tried to raise US$950,000 through crowdfunding and reached their target in under eight hours! In the end, more than US$8 million was raised and the console went on sale for US$99 in 2013.

SOURCING A SEQUEL

Psychonauts was a 3D platform game involving the character Raz as he becomes a psychic spy. It was a critical success and has become a cult classic but it only sold around 100,000 copies. Tim Schafer, the game's director, managed to raise US$3.8 million in 2016 to enable work to continue on its successor, Psychonauts 2.

SENTRIS

Some crowdfunding targets are more modest. Samantha Kalman's first full video game, Sentris, sees players drop musical notes from different instruments onto rings to create looping sounds. She raised US$6,361 above her target of US$50,000 in 2013 and the game was released for PlayStation 4, Linux, Windows and Apple OS X the following year.

Star Citizen features many different types of spaceship, including Hornets designed for dogfighting with other ships, and Freelancers, which specialize in trade and exploration.

COLLECT THEM ALL

Lots of people like to collect computer games, but some take it to a whole new level. Australia's Joel Hopkins has spent 20 years gathering games from all over the world. By 2016, his collection had grown to an incredible 18,000 – the biggest gathering of games in the world.

PLAY ROOMS

Joel Hopkins first played computer games using an Atari VCS in the late 1970s. His passion for gaming continued and saw him open a video game store in the early 1990s. Purpose-built rooms in his Melbourne home contain around 200 consoles, 43 of which are hooked up to TVs or monitor screens so that a selection of his enormous collection of games can be played. Joel uses his Last Gamer YouTube channel to keep his audience of more than 19,000 subscribers up to date on his games-collecting exploits.

NUMBERS GAME

The previous record holder was Michael Thomasson from New York. In 2012, an official count revealed he owned 10,607 different titles, including 725 games for PlayStation 2 alone. Around 2,600 of the games in his collection, which was started in the early 1980s, are still in their original shrink-wrapping and are unplayed.

MASSIVE MERCHANDISE

Brett Martin, from Colorado, USA, began his collection of gaming memorabilia when he was just eight. By 2014 he had built up a collection of 8,030 different items from giant statues of famous gaming characters to pillows, plush toys and even a Super Mario Bros Mario and Luigi shower head. Brett set up an online museum called the Video Game Memorabilia Museum to showcase his collection.

Record breaker Joel Hopkins poses in one of his customized gaming rooms.

NINTENDO GAME GATHERING

A policeman from the United Arab Emirates is believed to have the world's biggest collection of Nintendo-related items. Ahmed bin Fahad has gathered together over 8,000 Nintendo items including consoles, toys and every single edition of the Super Mario family of games.

GAMESCOM

If you think the biggest video games convention would be held in the gaming powerhouse nations of the USA or Japan, you'd be wrong. Gamescom in the German city of Cologne is the current record holder with a staggering 345,000 visitors attending both the 2015 and 2016 events.

BIGGER AND BIGGER

Since it began in 2009, Gamescom has grown and grown to become the centre of the European gaming industry. In 2016, 6,000 journalists came to cover the convention, which featured a whopping 877 different video game and associated companies.

FIRST LOOK

Part of the attraction for visitors is to get a first glimpse of major new games. Amongst the games making their debut at Gamescom 2015 were Guitar Hero Live, FIFA 16, Star Wars: Battlefront and the Legion expansion pack for World of Warcraft.

COSPLAY

Gamescom has its own dedicated area for cosplay fans which features celebrated manga artists and costume designers, photo booths and even a repair station to expertly fix any damaged costumes.

TOKYO GAME SHOW

The biggest gaming convention in Japan is held in Tokyo every September. In 2016, it recorded its highest ever attendance of 271,224 visitors, who checked out games from 614 exhibitors.

GAMESCOM AWARDS DATA

GAMESCOM ISSUES ITS OWN AWARDS DURING THE CONVENTION. HERE ARE SOME OF 2016's WINNERS.

Best of Gamescom	The Legend of Zelda: Breath of the Wild
Best Racing Game	Forza Horizon 3
Best Simulation Game	NBA 2K17
Best Strategy Game	Sid Meier's Civilization VI
Best Family Game	Skylanders Imaginators
Best Mobile Game	Mario Party Star Rush
Best Role-Playing Game	Final Fantasy XV

LIVE STREAM

The Electronic Entertainment Expo (E3) is a tradeshow for industry insiders only, but it is avidly followed by gamers for news of new games, consoles and features. In 2014, Twitch TV live streamed video from the four-day convention and attracted a record audience of 12 million viewers.

COSPLAY

In 2012, Tampere in Finland was the location of the first Angry Birds Land theme park. In September the following year, 491 people gathered at the park. All of them were dressed as video game characters such as Mario, Lara Croft and characters from Minecraft. It set the world record for the most cosplay characters in the one place.

The previous record was set in 2011 when 425 people dressed up as characters such as Luigi, Wario, Angry Birds and characters from Street Fighter and Pokémon at the headquarters of a costume company – Buyseasons in Wisconsin, USA.

 COSPLAY COMPETITIONS

Initially popular in Japan, but later spreading around the world, cosplayers dress up to look just like their favourite game characters. There are even championships all over the world to decide whose outfit is the very best. The World Cosplay Summit, held in Nagoya, Japan, welcomed competitors from 28 different countries in 2015.

This young Batman fan was part of a huge crowd of 470 people who gathered on 5 May 2012 in Federation Square, Melbourne, all dressed as video game characters.

Irish engineer Julian Checkley has produced an accurate replica Batman costume from the game Batman: Arkham Origins which is printed out using a 3D printer. The suit features folding batarangs and video screens fitted into the hand gauntlets!

Sonic at the 2013 E3 Electronic Entertainment Expo.

SUMMER OF SONIC

In 2006, a website was set up by Sven Joscelyne celebrating 15 years since the release of the first game featuring Sonic the Hedgehog. Two years later, the first Summer of Sonic Convention was held in Covent Garden, London. Fans of all things Sonic got to meet, check out costumes and secure a pre-release play of the Sonic game Sonic Chronicles.

BLIZZCON

More than 11,000 fans flock to BlizzCon each year at the Anaheim Convention Center in California to see the latest StarCraft and World of Warcraft creations. The convention also hosts live music and bands who have played at BlizzCon include Metallica, the Foo Fighters and Linkin Park.

PLENTY OF PERIPHERALS

Move over humble gamepads and joysticks, the world of gaming has seen some outrageous and odd gaming peripherals over the years. Imagine motion-sensitive fishing rods, electronic maracas and even entire robots.

GO FISH

Built to play Sega Bass Fishing on the Dreamcast console, this fishing rod handle and reel vibrates if a fish is caught during the game. Oddly, the controller is also compatible with the Virtua Tennis sports game!

MARACA MUSIC

Shake these electronic maracas to score points by matching the rhythms of the Samba de Amigo game. It was originally released for the Sega Dreamcast.

SHOUT IT OUT

The Konami LaserScope is a light gun worn on the head. You fire it not by pressing a button, but by shouting 'FIRE!' into the device's microphone. The peripheral also contains an eyepiece with crosshairs to help gamers aim at targets.

FOAM DARTS

A number of peculiar peripherals have been produced for Nintendo's Wii console. These include an American football inside which a games controller can be fitted and the NERF N-Strike, a fully working NERF gun that fires foam darts but also accepts a Wii controller for use with games.

GLOVE UP

The bulky, heavy NES Powerglove features sensors on the knuckles which communicate with sensors fitted to a TV. Around 100,000 Powergloves were sold from 1989 onwards, but only two games were produced specially for Powerglove use – a maze game called Super Glove Ball and a fighting game, Bad Street Brawler.

ROBOT PERIPHERAL

Who wouldn't like a robot pal that you control and that interacts with the game you're playing on-screen? Many agreed in the 1980s and bought Nintendo's Robotic Operating Buddy or R.O.B. for short. The 24cm (9.5in) tall robot can move its arms but is dreadfully slow.

BONKERS BONGOS

Donkey Konga was a 2003 game for the Nintendo GameCube where players have to play in time with music rhythms using a pair of electronic bongos. The crazy game was popular enough to spawn two sequels and a platform game using the bongos to move the in-game character left and right. You can also make the in-game character jump by hitting both bongos at the same time.

R.O.B. has since become a character in a number of other video games including Kirby's Dream Land 3, the Mario Kart series and Super Smash Bros. for Nintendo 3DS and Wii U.

TIMELINE 1950s-1980s

1961-2
Steve Russell and others at MIT create Spacewar! - the first computer action game featuring two battling spaceships.

1971
Computer Space, an arcade game designed by Nolan Bushnell and Ted Dabney, becomes the first computer arcade game built and played in relatively large numbers.

1972
Atari release their first video game for arcades - the tennis bat and ball game called Pong.

06 08

PONG

1977
The Atari Video Computer System (also known as the Atari 2600) goes on sale. It offers full colour gaming, different games on cartridges and paddle and joystick controllers.

1980
Namco introduces Pac-Man into arcades. It is a smash hit that offers players the chance to put their initials by their high scores and it is quickly ported to home games consoles.

1958
Scientist Willy Higinbotham invents a simple tennis game that uses an oscilloscope as a display at the Brookhaven National Laboratory in the USA.

1969
ARPANET, the forerunner of the Internet, goes online for the first time with just a handful of computers linked to one another.

1972
The Magnavox Odyssey, originally designed by Ralph Baer in the late 1960s, goes on sale as the world's first home gaming console.

1975
William Crowther writes Colossal Cave Adventure, the first text adventure game for computers.

1978
The highly influential Space Invaders arcade game is released for the first time. Its levels of gameplay, continuous soundtrack and high score feature make it a hit with gamers.

1983

The first of the series of Nintendo Entertainment System (NES) games consoles, also known as the Famicom, goes on sale in Japan.

1987

The very first Final Fantasy game debuts in Japan. The Final Fantasy series popularizes graphic role-playing games all over the world.

1985

Nintendo release Super Mario Bros, a multi-level platform game featuring Mario, a character who has since appeared in more than 200 other games.

1989

Nintendo launches its first Game Boy portable games console. Game Boys go on to become the most popular handheld games machine with hundreds of titles available to play.

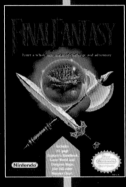

1982

Home computing booms with the release of colour home computers such as the Commodore 64 and the ZX Spectrum. Amateur programmers create hundreds of games for these and other machines.

1982

Microsoft Flight Simulator 1.0 is released whilst the Twin Galaxies database of record high scores in video games is published.

1981

IBM release their first PC (personal computer) whilst the first successful platform game Donkey Kong also goes on sale.

1984

Alexey Pajitnov creates the highly popular falling puzzle block game called Tetris. The game goes on to find its way onto almost every games console and platform since.

1986

The Legend of Zelda is introduced to the world and pioneers a game saving feature which allows gamers to carry on the game where they left off at a later date.

1988

The Sega Megadrive (called the Sega Genesis in the US) is released together with its six-button game controller, which proves influential for other game systems.

TIMELINE 1990s-2010s

1993
First-person shooter game Doom is launched by iD Software. With its realistic 3D environment and multiplayer gaming possibilities, it becomes very popular and influential.

1994
Sony launches its first PlayStation – a games console that uses compact discs to store games on rather than cartridges.

1996
Lara Croft debuts in the original Tomb Raider game for the Sony PlayStation, PC and the Sega Saturn console.

2000
The Sims goes on sale for the first time and becomes a popular and influential life simulation game.

2004
World of Warcraft is released and becomes the world's most popular MMORPG.

1991
Sonic the Hedgehog debuts in the platform game of the same name and becomes Sega's mascot, just like Mario is Nintendo's mascot.

1994
The Entertainment Software Rating Board is established to give ratings for games, similar to those used in movies, based on violence and other adult themes.

1995
The very first Electronic Entertainments Expo (E3) is held in Los Angeles in May. Over time, it becomes one of the largest computer gaming trade fairs in the world.

1997
Ultima Online pioneers many of the features of Massively Multiplayer Online Role Playing Game (MMORPGs) that are now taken for granted. It proves a hit and attracts over 100,000 paying gamers in less than six months.

2001
Microsoft enters the games console market with the Xbox. It is the first major games console to contain an internal hard disk drive.

2017

Nintendo releases its latest console, the Switch. With two removable Joy-Con games controllers, it can be played at home on a TV or on the move in handheld mode.

2011

Nintendo launch their Wii U console and the Nintendo 3DS handheld, whilst Sony releases its new-generation handheld console the PlayStation Vita.

2009

Angry Birds is released by Rovio. Gamers fire birds at naughty pigs and this simple game sparks a massive interest in fun games on smartphones and tablets.

2014

Microsoft buy Mojang, the company who produce Minecraft, for a figure of US$2.5 billion.

2005

The original Guitar Hero game is released by RedOctane and sparks a boom in music rhythm game machines.

2006

Nintendo introduces the Wii console with its motion-sensitive Wii remote controller and multiplayer games. It quickly becomes a hit with families and casual gamers.

2013

Sony release the PlayStation 4 console which includes a share button allowing players to view other gamers' play.

2004

Sony announces the PlayStation 2 has become the first games console to sell 100 million units worldwide.

2010

The Kinect motion-sensing device for Xbox 360 is released. It controls the game by monitoring a player's body movements and voice commands.

2016

ThePlayStation VR is released - a virtual reality headset allowing gamers to emerge themselves in 3D gameworlds. The Oculus Rift VR headset is also released.

GLOSSARY

3D printer
A device that creates physical objects from computer files by 'printing' repeated layers of material to build up a three dimensional (3D) object.

Adventure
A game genre in which the player follows a story, solves puzzles and explores the game's world.

Android
An operating system commonly found on smartphones and tablets.

App
A small computer program such as a game that can be downloaded and used on mobile devices like tablets and smartphones.

Arcade game
This originally meant games that were played on dedicated coin-operated machines in arcades and other public places. It has also become known as a genre of games with fast action that need quick reactions from gamers.

Bug
An error or fault in the code of a computer game that produces an unexpected result.

Clones
Copies or versions of an original game, sometimes without permission from the original game makers.

Console
A dedicated machine for playing games which connects to a display monitor or TV screen.

Controller
The device gamers use to perform actions and commands in a game. Common controllers include a mouse, joystick and gamepad.

Cosplay
Short for costume play, this is the hobby of dressing up as a character from a video game.

Dialogue
The words spoken by characters in a computer game.

Downloading
To obtain a computer file or program such as a game from another computer often by connecting to it over the Internet.

Easter eggs
Secret objects or features hidden inside video games, such as messages, mini-games or scenes.

eSports
Short for electronic sports – video game competitions and tournaments often held in front of live audiences which are also sometimes broadcast over the Internet.

Expansion pack
An add-on to a game which offers new game areas, game characters or objects and often extends the game's storyline and quests for the gamer to go on.

First-person game
A type of game where the gamer's point of view is as if through the eyes of the main game character.

Game Boy
A series of handheld game consoles, designed and built by Japanese company Nintendo, that proved very popular.

Gamepad
A type of game controller held in two hands with many buttons and usually either arrow buttons or mini joysticks to control direction in a game.

GB (gigabyte)
A measure of memory space equal to 1,000 megabytes. Hard disk drives are usually measured in hundreds or thousands of GB capacity.

Graphics card
A collection of chips and circuits on a board that help give a computer or digital device its ability to display images such as the fast-moving scenes in games.

Hard disk drive
A device found in many computers and some games consoles which stores information on a series of thin discs known as platters.

iOS
An operating system produced by the Apple company for use on its mobile devices such as iPads and iPhones.

Joystick
A lever that can be moved in a number of directions to control movement in a game such as moving a game character left or right or aiming a gun sight at a target.

Kinect
A motion-sensing device used with Xbox consoles allowing games to be played by moving your body without holding a games controller.

MB (megabyte)
A measure of memory storage equal to 1,000 kilobytes.

MMORPG
Short for Massively Multiplayer Online Role Playing Game, these are multiplayer games allowing thousands of gamers to play in the game's world connected via the Internet or another computer network.

Operating system
Computer programs which run a computer's basic functions and manage other programs running on the system.

Peripheral
A device such as a joystick, mouse, keyboard or printer which connects to a computer.

Platform games
Also known as platformers, these are games set in a vertical or 3D environment where characters advance by overcoming obstacles, moving and jumping on floors or platforms and, often, battling or avoiding enemies.

PlayStation
The name given to a line of games consoles produced by Sony including the PlayStation 4 and the PlayStation Portable (PSP) - a handheld console.

Port
The transfer of a game from one console or computer system to another. This often involves re-writing the game's program code so that it will work well on the new system.

RAM
Short for Random Access Memory, a type of computer memory that can store information and be rewritten.

Sandbox
Type of game which does not have one target or goal at the end. Instead, it is open-ended and allows gamers to roam through the world freely. Minecraft is a famous example of a sandbox game.

Sequel
A follow-up game to a previous game that often uses or develops the original game's themes, gameplay and characters.

Simulation game
Games that try to closely mimic or simulate real-world situations with as much realism and accuracy as possible.

Stream
To send a constant flow of data over a computer network to play video or music.

Stylus
A pencil-like object used to press on the touchscreens of tablets and handheld games consoles to perform commands.

TB (terabyte)
A measure of memory equal to 1,000 gigabytes. Some really big games take up terabytes of memory storage.

Trackball
A special controller that contains a ball that you roll with your fingers or palm of your hand.

Wii
A popular games console released by Nintendo in 2006 featuring handheld motion controllers and a large range of mostly family-friendly games.

Xbox
The name given to the line of games consoles produced by Microsoft including the Xbox 360 and Xbox One.

INDEX

The publishers would like to thank the following sources for their kind permission to reproduce the pictures in this book.

PHOTOGRAPHIC CREDITS
8-9, 9. (top right), 9. (bottom left) Evan-Amos, 10. Brookhaven National Laboratory, 11. Evan-Amos (top centre), Private Collection (top right), Evan-Amos (centre), 12. Joi Ito (centre), JohnsJukes (bottom), 14. Chris Wilson/Alamy Stock Photo, 14-15. ArcadeImages/Alamy Stock Photo. 15. Lisa Plevey/Stockimo/Alamy Stock Photo (top right), Zuma Press, Inc./Alamy Stock Photo (bottom right), 16. Simon Tang/REX/Shutterstock, 16-17. ArcadeImages/Alamy Stock Photo, 18. 8Pack, 19. VRX Ventures Ltd. (top) 19. Evan-Amos (bottom right), 21. Drew Angerer/Getty Images (bottom right), 23. Shutterstock (top right), 24. Lynne Sutherland/Alamy Stock Photo, 25. Franck Fife/AFP/Getty Images (top left), Stefano Tinti/Shutterstock.com (top right), Maurice Savage/Alamy Stock Photo (bottom right), 27. Mario Tama/Getty Images (top), Chesnot/Getty Images (bottom), 31. SWNS.com (bottom right), 32-33. David Caudery/Future Publishing/REX/Shutterstock, 33. DPA Picture Alliance Archive/Alamy Stock Photo (top right), 34. Evan-Amos (bottom), 34. TinyCircuits.com (centre), 35. Jason Camerbis, 36. John Phillips/UK Press via Getty Images, 37. Private Collection (top), Mad Catz (left), MWE Lab (bottom right), ColorWare (bottom), 38. Buzz Foto/REX/Shutterstock (top), Albert L. Ortega/Getty Images (bottom), 38-39. AF Archive/Alamy Stock Photo, 39. Aaron Davidson (top right), (centre) New Line/Everett/REX/Shutterstock, 40-41. Shutterstock.com, 43. Ryan Anson/AFP/Getty Images (bottom right), Shutterstock.com (centre right), 44. ClassicStock/Alamy Stock Photo, 45. & 45 (bottom right) ArcadeImages/Alamy Stock Photo, 46. Richard Lautens/Toronto Star via Getty Images (bottom left), Snap/REX/Shutterstock (centre), 47. Paul Archuleta/FilmMagic/Getty Images (right), 48. David Lee/Alamy Stock Photo (bottom left), Donald Bowers/Getty Images for Guinness World Records, 53. (top right) Rebecca Andrews/REX/Shutterstock, 54-55. NASA, 54. (left) & 55. (top) Shutterstock.com, Ian T. Edwards (right), SSPL/Getty Images (bottom left), Kos_Duo (bottom right), 57. Jorge Gonzalez/Pacific Press/LightRocket via Getty Images (bottom right), 59. JHPhoto/Alamy Stock Photo (top), Incamerastock/Alamy Stock Photo (right), www.segaretro.org (left), 60-61. Kevin Britland/Alamy Stock Photo, 60. Shutterstock.com (centre), Ian Dagnall Computing/Alamy Stock Photo, 62-63. John Shearer/WireImage/Getty Images, 65. Louis Lanzano/Bloomberg via Getty Images (top), 73. KeystoneUSA-ZUMA/REX/Shutterstock, 80. Courtesy of Ryan Hart (left), 81. & 83. Shutterstock.com (right), 84. Fabrice Coffrini/AFP (left), VfL Wolfsburg (bottom), 85. Alexander Hassenstein - FIFA/FIFA via Getty Images, 86. Kai Hendry, 87. The Asahi Shimbun via Getty Images (top), John Lamparski/Getty Images (bottom right), 88-89. & 89t. SeongJoon Cho/Bloomberg via Getty Images, David Williams/Bloomberg via Getty Images (bottom), 92. David L. Ryan/The Boston Globe via Getty Images (bottom), 92-93. ZUMA Press, Inc./Alamy Stock Photo, 93. Toru Yamanaka/AFP/Getty Images (top), 96-97. Jeff Crow/Edge Magazine via Getty Images, 97. Craig F. Walker/The Denver Post (top), Shutterstock.com (bottom), 98-99 Photo Koelnmesse, 100. Neilson Barnard/Getty Images (bottom), 100-101. Quinn Rooney/Getty Images, 101. Albert L. Ortega/Getty Images (right), Kamil Krawczak (centre), Ricardo DeAratanha/Los Angeles Times via Getty Images (bottom), 102. Private Collection, 103. Evan-Amos (left & bottom).

Every effort has been made to acknowledge correctly and contact the source and/or copyright holder of each picture and Carlton Books Limited apologises for any unintentional errors or omissions that will be corrected in future editions of this book.

SPECIAL ACKNOWLEDGEMENTS
2K Sports, Activision Publishing, Atari, Blizzard, Bioware, CAPCOM, CCP Games, Cloud Imperium Games Corporation & Roberts Space Industries Corp, Codemasters, Dota2, Double Fine Productions, Electronic Arts, Epic Games, Facebook, King.com, Konami, Lucasfilm Entertainment, Microsoft Studios, MIT, NERF, Nintendo, Rovio, Sega, SSCE, Square Enix, Squad, Tetris Press, Timbre Interactive, Ubisoft, Ultimate Play the Game, Valve Corp, Xbox, Warner Bros Interactive Games.